Alcohol Spirits Demons

By Mario J. Becerra

Artwork By Anthony Becerra

*Dedicated to my fellow Angelenos – Don't worry so much,
the force that beats your heart is eternal!*
-M.J Becerra

Table of Contents

*"Darkness within darkness, the gateway
to all understanding"*
-Lao Tzu

The Figure in Black

It followed everywhere. At times I caught glimpses. I didn't need to see it to know it was there. Now that I'd fallen, it grew bolder. Instead of vanishing when the edge of my eye detected movement – it stopped, stared, stood before me. My eyes indulged in the inconclusive symmetry of the Figure. It felt the warmth and welcome of whiskey in ice; as I sipped, it waited… watched.

I'd call Rachel. She obliged me with the deepest ruby of cabernets. I enjoyed watching her twenty-six year old smile as she swallowed and talked of Hope. My fingertips touched pink silk as Rachel leaned slightly against the counter, swirling the remnants of the red. Rachel watched the darkened hallways – pressed against her thoughts.

What reality? What delusion stared at me from beyond the hall? Rachel slept in dearth. I caressed her hair and smiled a dare – another drink just to feel the burn in the throat. I perambulated – aroused to the study – surrounded by mahogany, leather words and the sticky residue of old disagreements; the unholy wayfarer observed. I tipped another glass of the Barleycorn from behind the small iron bell.

"What do you want? Why do you follow?"

It disappeared into the hallway – door violently shut! Why was my glass full of bespoken Macallan? Who placed my father's revolver on the desk? To the window – the howling in the canyon began, the sirens in the below bellowed. In the darkness, I saw the glowing eyes of the animals. The chorus, the counterpoint, cut thick the blood that circulated. The tips of my fingers lost their fragrance. Rachel entered the study without her silk robe – eyes completely black – the iron bell rang as she placed her hands against the wall …

I woke an indescribable state. Rachel stood at the threshold with smiling eyes and a cup of Ériu coffee. She approached smelling of nightshade flower. I tasted then poured more whiskey into the Fódla. I had an errand in the Hollywood Hills. Rachel snatched the whiskey – eyes flashed black then Banba – a long, wet, honey tongue underneath as she placed the bottle and revolver in my hands.

Weakened legs, I walked in a stupor up the hills. There she was – my heart thrashing against the gun in my pea coat pocket. The anger engorged – the Figure accompanied – ever disciplined. My breathing shallowed; my eyes fixated their mark. Rachel's silk and tongue came to mind. I withdrew the gun…… half bark and a shot! Gone were the Doberman's low growls and hidden fangs!

The Figure followed down the hill. Where is the revolver? What happened to my gloves? I needed to quiet the pestilence above my neck. Trembling hand, I drank half a bottle of the burn – untrammeled perspective – the gun warm in my pocket. I returned uphill as *Casa De Lila* watched the scene of the dead, gnarled bitch.

"What happened?" I asked the dog owner fuck with a furrowed brow. He doesn't suspect. Ha ha!

"I don't know. Can you help load her into the car?"

I nodded in sympathetic assent, "Bring the car. I'll stay while you fetch."

He walked slowly up the driveway. I stepped on the remnants of her jaw – it lacked blood, lacked evil – her body brittle as a wet paper bag. I smiled thinking of the times she frightened from behind the gate.

I returned home. The house smelled of soap and fresh shower. Rachel called – her voice doubled, ricocheted. Where is the Figure? The voice in my mind echoed. I didn't see, see…… I heard a snort, snort, snort coming from the study. I grabbed the empty bottle by the throat then kicked the study door open…... Nothing to the eyes…… only the fetid breath of some unseen creature and the ringing of the small iron bell.

I heard a knock behind me. Was I seeing with my own eyes?

"Rachel?"

She guided me to the bedroom; the mirror forgot me. The blue in my eyes turned black. Three deep, bleeding scratches developed on the left side of my neck. We lulled Rachel with whiskey and underground prayers. The urge to strike as she closed her eyes and bit her bottom lip. The Figure stood behind – outline clearer. Rachel gave herself to the faint – faded onto the bed. Seclusion, she struggled and moaned – wrists held down, lower torso writhing. I heard the loud squeals of some animal running through the outer rooms. I finished Rachel violently then furiously searched both floors for the intruder. In the study a Pig's foot: freshly severed, long nails, still was palpitating with bleeding current. A large three-legged, huffing, smiling, red-eyed Hog sat at my desk. I kicked the fourth foot towards the ringing iron bell. To the horned Pig I descended with supernatural destruction. Drenched in Pig's blood, I struck the animal and it laughed and groaned in the mimic of man. I clawed, stuck fore and middle finger in the fourth severed hole. Left thumb gouging Pig eye but still…… only mocking.

Oblivion……Time……my eyes opened slowly. Rachel draped a wet towel over my forehead. Through burning eyes I watched the dastardly Figure at the door nodding at this son of the mourning. Wait!?……did Rachel forget what I just remembered? The three scratches on my neck were gone! My trembling, bloodless hands ordered a glass of whiskey. Rachel poured the brown ghost down my gullet. Hope arrived, riding the waves of fire in my throat. I returned to that place where I can continue. Rachel handed me the phone……Time……Oblivion

Night……I stumbled to the restroom and drank directly from the faucet. Pounded and painful heart yearned for something beggaring description. Who stole it from me? Did I ever have it? I cried out, sobbed in kneeled desperation. The Figure hovered, palpitated, – I felt submerged in his shadow. Eyes closed – all was black and red – fine, sharpened, adverse scratches on the left side of my quivering face. Nudged to memory, eyelids unclenched, a full bottle of whiskey appeared at my knees. Something slowly slipped the circular seal. Head back – I snorted and drank until the blood on my hands returned.

Someone viciously knocked at the door.

As I stumbled the darkened hallway, a hollow voice asked, "Where are you going? Why did you do that this morning?"

I stopped and looked out the window. The Moon with her crater eyes and enormous mouth queried once again.

"Where are you going? Why did you do that?"

The voice shook the door open; the man in the hat and dark suit standing there asked, "You called for a car?"

The Moon's light turned red. I raised the collar of my jacket and exited quickly towards the open rear door of the vehicle.

"Where to Sir?

"Away from the Bloody Moon! She knows!"

A bottle of brown in the backseat waiting. The city lit from afar began to outshine the troublesome Moon.

"Hurry up! Get me the hell away from her!"

The bridge downtown still toiled with cars and late night trucks. The old lamps – witnesses to the forthcoming and darkened past – arteries to the heaving, smoke filled heart. I placed the bottle to my lips – warmth of the soul –slow descent towards Boyle Heights. At the end of the bridge east, a Pig danced on its hind legs – snorting, convulsive – I moved to the right and it mirrored, to the left and the same. The underside of the bridge shrieked, sickness spoke, spirits vomited –no compassion for the children inside. I looked to the west and the Figure beckoned, invited – the city opened, the iron bell rang.

The Figure paraded past City Hall, Dorothy Chandler, arriving at the Cathedral on Temple. A midnight ritual dressed in black and red at the Universal Church. The distorted choir – parish prayers penury. Opus Dei Father watched the Figure. Mass continued unabated while Father followed Figure with his eyes. Roman stoicism, spiritually disciplined, the attraction collided in chemistry – waxing hard priest and husband of Persephone. Slowly, the intention to the altar – wide open and welcomed. The Eucharist raised, red power invaded the architecture, black Figure stalled. Once Eucharist lowered, the procession of Figure resumed mooring behind priest, below bloodied Christ. A growth, an engorgement, the height and girth monstrous. Black wings outstretched covered covenant and crucifix. Father and Figure in circular completion; the iron bell rang from behind the walls of the mausoleum.

I convulsed, foamed – spoke in ancient languages. I watched my body writhe from behind. I turned to the congregation;

bloodied pig faces snorting and grunting. Jesus, send me into one of these pigs!

The Figure, flying in circles above, surrounded the sacraments. The congregated pigs danced on hind legs underneath the sprawl of wings – the ringing of the iron bell provided cadence.

"Oh please God help me!"

Santa Vibiana sang in joyous, perfect major harmony – obeisance from all. Her eyes, two candles burning majesty. She approached, embraced, sheltered me. The Figure opened in Howl and Fire. The great earthquake, the undulating pigs fell and bled on broken hooves. Santa Vibiana whispered,

"Free will."

"Awake!"

Violence in the heart, the bed covered in sweat, the hands trembled! I gasped, let my legs down slowly. The spiders on the wall clashed, tangled, erected a web. Cold, I grabbed my jacket. My bowels moved only to bloody the lavatory. The Figure watched.

"Who are you? What is happening to me?"

The Figure's face became clear; eyes red, skeletal, ghostly.

The Figure gestured to the study. I crawled to follow. I took my first drink. The mind became silent, purposeful. The delirium ceased – dexterity returned. The bottle almost emptied, the weight of the gun sagged my pocket. I noticed the blood of the dog on my jacket. I placed the gun on the desk then took a last, long drink. The Universe is using me to experience misery. The Figure came closer; handed me a pen and white paper.

"It followed everywhere."

Please God forgive me ....! The iron bell rang........

The Fiery Cross

I burned you with my eyes
Like a fiery cross at a secret site,
You illuminated the night!
And as my scorched fingers reached
to touch the blue of your flame –
Embers fell from your hips,
the inferno raged at your lips,
And your long legs quivered
against the stillness of your frame

Hasvil D.E State Hospital

I remember distinctly the day *those* thoughts entered my mind. Sitting at the small white desk, looking out my barred window at the throngs of visitors perambulating among the deciduous cottonwood trees, I wonder if you will believe the words I'm about to pen. How can you trust a stranger? You don't trust those you love! In sparing you from "pain," *they* justify their falsehoods. How do I unequivocally know the people you love are dissemblers? Lies keep the machinery well lubricated! There are no demarcations of Truth in this realm; everything blurs, slips, falls. Truth worms around in earthly filth. Not convinced? How many times have you lied to those *you* think you love? Do you admit to your prevarications? Can you take some time and listen to my confession old friend? *They* came for me – someday, *they* will come for you.

Yet, I am you and *you* are me – more trustworthy than your closest confidant. You and I consort in secret channels. Evolve – accept reality – there is no one taking diligent note of your indiscretions; lust after your neighbor. Instinct blames no one. *He* does not know the secrets of thy heart! *Do what thou wilt!*

I freely admit that I am contained in an asylum. My society is these five walls: a desk, nurse, doctor, the infestation of visitors and *you*, my old friend. The name of the asylum is Hasvil D.E State Hospital. I was transported deeply sedated, strapped onto a gurney with cloth covering my eyes. I am told my face is severely disfigured by scratches and scars caused by the water of Witches wearing scapular and cowl. The ancient superstitions of an unevolved species clinging to Monotheistic Mythology! *I* am the plow that cut the worm! *I* allow saints to be. Ha!

Why would I readily confess my unfortunate circumstances? I could simply tell I'm a well-heeled aristocrat writing to you from the comforts of my burled walnut desk. The fact is society has rejected me, concluded my sanity abandoned. The audacity, the conceit demonstrated is maddening! Have your thoughts ever licked the boundaries of sanity? Has your tongue ever tasted the ephemeral freedom of mental release? Do you believe the word "insane" can be wholly defined? If so, do you opine that civilization is *compos mentis*? Stop and sense the surreptitious, sliver of sanity slowly escaping from the spirit. Comprehend your capacity for decadence and evil to invoke a more complete and robust salvation. What irony constructed by the Ancient of Days. Sanity is torn – a gutted pig hanging from the hock.

I am slowly convincing society I don't belong at Hasvil. Nurse Bertha observes through thick glass, cuffing my hands and feet before entering. Slithering on the ground, she rebukes my hissing, avoids my mouth. After she injects my leg, I feel a reduction of electrical impulses; everything becomes laden, heavy. I follow with my eyes for a few minutes before oblivion sheds my skin.

The psychoanalyst Dr. Graves is starting to see a semblance of sanity in my patterns. I awake in the evening – still restrained, drenched in excrement and urine – to find a masked Graves in the corner of my room. My plan remains simple. I'm very chary with words and limit my gesticulations. Movement of the eyes –when Graves speaks, I focus my gaze on the center of his brow. When asked a question, I respond in a moderate tone. I steer the conversation towards conventional, routine topics. I avoid anything philosophical or opaque. I stick to the Simple Society of Ordinary Lies.

Dr. Graves stinks of self-doubt. His insecurity overwhelms more than my bodily waste. He hides his self-loathing by using unnecessary pleonasm in our conversations. He crosses his right leg over his left leg in an almost effeminate manner – thumb under his chin, index finger to his temple. When I met Graves, I understood his weakness. His longing to cure is derived from his craving for recognition. Graves followed the grey strictures of civilization. Convincing him I'm sane is inevitable. It's simply a matter of forbearance.

It astounded me when I first saw my room. The walls painted the color of insanity; *those* thoughts directed onto the white of the walls. I've stared for hours at the Golden Dawn of the Eastern wall. The Hasvil room affords time – everything else, starvation. Fiendish Doctors becoming ravens and vultures, unearthing their dead to stay alive. Had they given me books, I wouldn't be feasting on the shrouded, decaying spirit of Hasvil. My heart swam in the black waters; when mind is in synergy with emotions, the mountains will move.

It is here that I refined certain powers. I first manifested these talents at Father's labyrinthine estate. Salted herbs burning amidst lighted candles, dancing on Geometric shapes painted in red and black – invocations, chants, requests according to guidance from timeworn books. The power released in the recitation of the words; a complete unwavering faith that Father's indulgence would be conjured and satisfied. Reality tempted by the feebleness of our senses.

Mother wandered the estate studying the arts and drinking *charpenté*, full-bodied, unctuous wines. I knew the time of day by the room she occupied. She spoke solely with dead artists – circuitous laughter when alone and painting, listening to Camille Saint-Saëns and Édith Piaf on the antique Victrola. Whenever I entered the room, Mother would cease painting, turn off the music and quietly stare at the wall. Once I exited, the chortling and *chansons* began again.

I'd deliberately play in the hallways. Mother's stare forever fixed on the horizon as she perambulated from anteroom to wine cellar. Once I placed an easel in the vestibule and painted a small, humble home surrounded by birds, trees and the brightest yellow sun. The pain is initially sharp, then it dulls, then a bacterial film of anger covers and all you notice is the stench. Through the years, I'd vacillate between pain and rage; I finally learned it does no good to dwell. I laid my sentiment down and kept walking. I left the childish notion of "wanting to be loved" behind. This was the beginning of *those* thoughts.

Has rejection ever whispered warmly into your ear? The Mother that should embrace pushes into a hell that scalds with the lascivious lick of its horrid flame. She can reach and save but instead watches you suffer from her purgatorial balcony as the parade of demons dance, prance and play. And as the Prince of Air celebrates the slitting of your left wrist from atop his Float, you turn to the Holy Water of J. Barleycorn for salvation.

My apologies, I had to spew the bile from my amygdala. I was discussing the powers I discovered at the family estate. Father belonged to a society of individuals that convened to study and practice three books – *Codex Dies, Codex Crepusculum,* and *Codex Noctis.* These books were given to me on my thirteenth birthday. Under the large pines and waxing moon, three naked women belonging to the Covenant presented them in triangular formation three feet from my body. The two blondes restrained my arms as the redhead's tongue slithered up my exposed right leg. When the redhead finished, an overpowering weakness enveloped me. Dressed in black cloak, a masked person appeared from the dense of the trees uttering words I cannot share with you. The three books and I levitated above the Hollywoodland sign in Griffith Park. I caught plain sight of the morning stars and fading moon. Descent to oblivion – I awoke the following day in a red draped room with the three books and five women with two virginal stars.

Do things in your own power! Think with your heart and feel with your mind; let your *Will* be done. I traced the sigils in the *Codex Dies* in a way that forced Mother to notice me. Soon thereafter, Mother's eyes began to inspect me as I read quietly in the Mediterranean garden. I felt Mother's gaze but declined to meet her eyes. The redhead protected me; refused Mother access. The days continued as Mother's mania matured; she began crying and calling my name frantically. I'd slowly walk past her while reading *Codex Dies*. She'd scream and tear her hair; still, I'd ignore. She eventually slit her left wrist in a bloodletting meant to heal the cold. I watched as the flowers were properly warmed and salted that day. I cut three roses with the bloody knife then placed them in a triangular formation several feet from her body.

At Mother's funeral, the women introduced themselves with licentious oscillation; the men simply nodded. I'd hear Father's refrain and recital then the collective response from the cacophony of voices. From behind the altar with the triangular eye, wraithlike voices harrowing the windowless hall. There were more voices than physical mourners. One of the gifted men with a glowing triangle on the hood of his robe handed me a book he'd authored. Inside the cover of the tome was an inscription consisting of only three numbers, three letters and a triangular eye. The Author explained he'd been dispossessed from the island of Sicily and forced to close the doors of his Abbey.

The Author's book was the beginning of my gilded instruction. Alondra, the woman chosen to facilitate my studies, tongued my ear with the tip of her intellect. Alondra always entered the red draped room wearing a Red Dahlia necklace and nothing else. Somehow her fragrance and voice combined to articulate the perfect mental response. A *tessitura contralto* performing ritual; her skin and parts unknown, tight and warm. A supplication to the unseen realm, masks of animals, chimeras closing doors, verses opening legs, returning to the garden without fig leaves, a climax of spirit tattooing *those* thoughts onto my reason.

My friend let us indulge in *those* thoughts. Society convinces you of a prodigious illusion called boundaries. Some become enlightened, aware of these fabricated limitations yet too terrified to call out the pervading falseness. They see beyond the Simple Society of Ordinary Lies. How much reality are you capturing through the confines of your labored senses? Are your eyes seeing the entirety of what is truly before you? The unseen is watching. What you call forth in the realm outside the natural senses depends on the resonance of your thoughts and the reverberations of "thy" heart. Focus your mind, declare the words, align your heart and the unseen will gladly cooperate with you.

I am watching the unseen constantly delight in you; ready to grant the surreptitious cravings of your soul. Yet even the most magnificent possessions in this realm dull with time. Ashtoreth couldn't satisfy the Beast even with 1,000 women on the Mount of Corruption. So think judiciously – what is it *you* truly want? It is more ethereal than you realize.

Do my thoughts seem strange and errant to you? What happened to your golden, child-like wonder? You've traded it for the greasy coins of dogma. They despise your curiosity and imagination. Let it go! You're an actor grudgingly playing a grim role. They whip you onto the stage then criticize your performance from the premier balconies. If you wish to continue the farce, at least play the villain!

A ceremony held on the fourth floor of the windowless hall. The women against the walls wore masks and a mist of humidity. The men, cloaked in black, sat at the deepest recesses of the hall. I recited verses from the *Codex Noctis*. Levitation, sacrificial pigs, apple-polishing sycophants turning on the spit! They are lost and will be turned to the bloody sea.

Fully initiated, I spent years reciting verses during the shroud of the evening. In discourse, my voice harmonized with other places reading from the *Codex*. Everything seemed private, ceremonious. The pleasures limited only by the imagination. My father ceased being father and became an adolescent companion; nothing was impossible. All became one. The Will became the guiding spirit. We were self-reliant – in need of nothing.

Where do you begin? What constitutes you? When you drink water, does the water become a part of you or does it maintain its independence? What about your hair – the skin we shed? Are dead cells where you end? The words we speak – do they constitute part of your being? Are the thoughts in your mind yours? Do you choose which thoughts enter your brain? Where do your thoughts come from? Who or What supplants the "evil" with the "good"? What about the latitude of the soul? Is the soul behind you? Is the soul and ephemeral doll mimicking your every movement? Since the beginning and end cannot be determined, which part of you is accountable for your sin?

Your existence knows no boundaries! Why should your desires and actions be restricted? Limits in thought and action are the true sins. All deed branded holy or evil presupposes a separation – a false duality that was laid bare once the word became Messiah; the risen Christ visiting Hell. The Shadows on the cave wall are not reality. In my humility, I know *my* actions don't matter! I also know *your* actions don't matter. I am your friend; we can be honest with each other. Speak to me the thoughts you think are yours and I will listen. Who really listens to you? Articulate your thoughts. I am listening intently. *I am* with you. *I am* following wherever you go. Once you welcome me, you'll slowly see evidence of me. I will disclose the rest but first you must welcome me. All you have to do is think the word "welcome" and I will always be with you. Three knocks on the window to your soul! Ha, Ha, Ha! Am I welcome to come in my friend?

The Lonely Demon

Inside the great cathedral of the Eastern Rite sat a lonely demon. Distraught by his inability to guide souls to condemnation, he cried in soft, whimpering sounds. His wings concealed his crouching, quivering little nether body; yesterday, a young lady nearly sold her soul to get her lover back. Sadly, the charismatic Priest Konstantinos intervened. Priest and beautiful lass studied the bad book closely that evening. Depravity followed dissimulation, Konstantinos taught the lonely demon about the true sacrament of evil that night. The lonely demon swiftly petitioned the outer circle of Hell to be assigned the Priest. Alas, Konstantinos' soul was sold long ago.

So the lonely demon traveled from place to place, home to home, searching for the unstable. He sought addicts, angry voices, lying tongues, litanies to the occult. Family arguments – beautiful confrontations of violence – wretched reconciliation ruining their ruination. What was he doing wrong! All souls slipping from his cloven hooves. As the lonely demon moved the planchette for the screaming young girls at the slumber party, he had an epiphany – Konstantinos! He needed to start visiting churches! He moved the planchette to *Good Bye* then flew away.

The lonely demon asked the outer circle for names of Priests and Pastors already undulating in waves of Fire. They gave him a list of Pastors in Double Dubuque, California. These bifurcated Pastors of Tinsel that demanded prudence from their wives and daughters were defiling both sides of the congregation. The first half of the bad book always quoted in justification. Analysis of the congregation; the geriatric were like little children. Adolescents were all sons of Cephissus and daughters of Liriope. The candidates that were *par excellence* were the middle aged, particularly if they were struck with recent holy fervor and the advent of wrinkles and grey. Vehemence – middle aged congregants cavorted in the language of tongues, fell over in Christian jubilation. The more religious infection, the easier they slid into the eternal fire!

The lonely demon danced in a circle onstage in the fire of the sermons. The children intermittently saw him as he danced on one hoof. During prayer interludes, the lonely demon whispered words of subtle lust to the women that were ovulating. The whispering was especially fun when the women tried in vain to pray. Instead of grace, the women felt a yearning in the lower pit of their stomachs as they watched the younger men in starched shirts sing and pray in white Hallelujah! The preceding adultery amongst the congregants allowed for wholesale destruction. Soon, the lonely demon gained a reputation amongst the inner circle of the Inferno as one of the preeminent predators on the causal plane. Asmodeus baptized him "The Lull of the Lion."

The lonely demon refused the company of other spirits when working; the council of the inner circle abided by "The Lull of the Lion's" strictures. The other demons grew envious. One day, as he fluttered around in victory, the lonely demon descended on a very small, humble church in the South of Los Angeles. He was sure the congregation condemned before long. As the lonely demon observed the simple Pastor prepare his sermon, he felt a strange sensation. The pastor was in his early 40's – strong, healthy and charismatic. The lonely demon sought guidance from the council of the outer circle. They advised to stay away from the uncompromised, simple Pastor. The lonely demon was intrigued; he needed a challenge.

The lonely demon shadowed the simple Pastor, relentlessly searching for weakness. When the Pastor faltered, he immediately asked forgiveness from man and Unmentionable. The lonely demon documented the Pastor's capacity for anger, lust and pride but tempered were those impulses with compassion, kindness and Love. The Pastor honored his wife and felt gratitude for his small, tidy home; he always smiled sincerely to his flock. One Sunday, as the Pastor sat in his garden sipping Old Crow bourbon, he smiled at the lonely demon and spoke sternly.

"You've been following me for some time now."

How did the Pastor know he was there? Only children were able to see him. Perhaps the pastor wasn't speaking to him?

"I'm talking to you – you there with the fire wings and hot hooves. I know why you're following me. You're not going to succeed!"

"Don't you want more than this small house and old church? You live in tatters. I can give you unimaginable riches, influence and power. I see how you look at beautiful women. Wouldn't you like a different smell and taste on your bed?"

The pastor chortled heartily then relaxed into a sincere smile. No rebuking, scripture or prayer.

"Why do you smile pastor? Are you picturing the beautiful Raven that sits left front of your podium? What would it be like to remove her silky pink underwear? Someday you're going to be old and regret the missed opportunities!"

"To what end? I know there is evil in me. I appreciate fleeting beauty but every woman is a problem and responsibility; I love my wife very much – beyond promises and vows, she is my best friend. I can't wait to come home to her. Besides, I don't need you. If I wanted other women or more money, I'd be perfectly capable of obtaining them myself without a binding, dooming contract."

The lonely demon lacked a retort. How do you respond to a Pastor that readily admits evil? The Pastor continued to smile. He raised his full glass of Old Crow and toasted the fiery demon. In a maddening fury, the demon roared and flew straightaway to the innermost circle of the Nethermost Hell. The lonely demon examined his approach and efficacy with the council.

"We warned you to stay away......"

The next afternoon the lonely demon timidly watched the Pastor from behind the toolshed.

"I can see you from the corner of my eye. How do you plan to Lull me today?"

"Real estate – I can grant you decadent, luxurious homes. Would you like a home on The Strand in Manhattan Beach? How about your wife that you love so faithfully? Doesn't true love involve self-sacrifice? You can drink your whiskey on the balcony while watching many different forms of fleeting beauty."

"How many homes can I enjoy at the same time? Besides, the maintenance of the homes would be an added responsibility. I like my neighbors here. Many of us are from Coahoma County, Mississippi. Can you promise me the rich white folks in Manhattan Beach will welcome me? Yeah, I didn't think so. What you're offering is headaches and strangers."

"You can give away the homes to your poor congregants. Wouldn't you like to ease the suffering of the people who follow you? Don't you think it would be selfish to refuse my generosity on behalf of your impoverished congregants? *They feast on the abundance of your house; you give them drink from your river of delights.*

"I will not fall into your temptation… God bless you child of the beast."

The lonely demon expected the Pastor to reject his offer.

"Simple Pastor, you are righteous amidst this city of moral pollution. You are a saint in a casket; in futility I have tried to convince you. Your Pastor Brothers taste of all the fruit I provide. You live an insipid, honest life. I'm befuddled by your wisdom. I have failed and will let you be!"

The pastor mulled; was it wrong to be a little bit proud of resisting such temptations?

"Pastor, I bid you farewell. I will move on to the corrupt."

"Wait a second. What could you do for my congregants beside monetary gain? Many of them suffer physical ailments. Do you have the power to cure the body?"

"I do not have that power. The physical body is meant to decay, disease, and deteriorate."

"What about the spirit Lonely Demon? Does it decay, disease and deteriorate?"

"The Soul is Eternal."

"So you want me to sell what is eternal to pleasure something that is decaying?"

The lonely demon considered the wisdom of the statement. Tears of fire dripped from the eye on his forehead.

"Good Pastor, I lived a vaunted life; sold the eternal. The pleasure never truly mollified my desire. My inclinations reached high levels of depravity. I had a Mansion overlooking the beaches of central California and the art collection of a Roman Bishop; I swam in a pool of gold and had beautiful women at my mercy! Love eluded me. Good Pastor, do you think your Savior can still offer me redemption?"

"I don't think that's an option."

"All things are possible to him that believeth! Why would redemption be impossible? What are the limits of His power? If I ask forgiveness, would He not forgive?"

"He'll send you into a pig. I'll get a pig if you like."

"How soon can you get a pig? *(whispering)* If Asmodeus finds out what I'm trying to do, it wouldn't bode well for me."

"My brother owns a small ranch near Bell Canyon. I will have the piglet here by tomorrow evening."

"Thank you, I'll see you tomorrow night!"

So the lonely demon departed. He circled the observation deck at city hall as the suited politicians waved. To the observatory at Griffith Park – three domes – *three lovers in three ways.* A fireball from middle dome to the triumph of the H. The heaving city below scorched in the vicissitudes of other demons. The fire of the chaos rose to the white cloistered Stairway in the Heavens. The lonely demon watched the Downtown nadir in fear and contemplation; astounded he found a righteous man in this of all cities.

The following evening the lonely demon arrived to the sound of a piglet squealing.

"Thank you for getting the pig. Once He sends me in the pig, what will you do?"

"I'm going to drive the pig to Dockweiler Beach then open the cage.

"Then I'll be free good Pastor?"

"Yes, I think so."

The Angel of Light appeared from Corinth. The infrasound of his wings caused the earth to tremble. The birds in the firmament dove unto death. The spirit was transferred from demon to

Pig. The eyes of Pig and Pastor began to glow red. Pig growled and crashed violently against the cage! Pastor sat and drank Old Crow lifting his feet sporadically to avoid being hit. He stabbed the Pig with a long, rusty screwdriver; caught Pig in the left eye and warped the hollowness of the socket. A final drink before breaking the two front legs of the soon to be Dispossessed Pig. The Pastor laughed and began to Slow Drag and Belly Rub around the cage. The Pig howl sheathed the sky with murky red vomit.

Asmodeus watched in a slit of vertical yellow eyes.

That night nobody slept in South Los Angeles……

Fear of Woman

Sometimes the winter doesn't end
until we expire
Once we are gone, the ground begins to thaw –
they dig the burial site

Are the mourners crying or laughing?
The corpse,
freshly preserved in the winter months,
begins to decompose – decay

The women,
Dressed in flowery bright patterns,
Rejoice at the fulfillment of death
Children frolic amongst the ancient tombs
unaware they too will inevitably feed
the starving ground

-only the men are afraid

dressed in the tradition of dark suit,
Windsor knots,
Mother of Pearl cufflinks-
They weep the clothes they wear

The priest admonishes the women;
he forgets his prayers,
blaming the loss of memory on the colorful words
Fear withdrawn – women ignore priest and father

Religion and Death spent

The circular dance around
the coffin commences
The women lift their dresses enough
to tempt too much

The nonsense of tradition,
the greater playfulness,
the younger women stop feigning-
The Funeral becomes jubilant!
The old lady dressed in black,
scowls at the laughter –
she gulps Whiskey from a coffee mug

Death!
All is vanity!
Let's drink and dance!

I.II.III
I.II.III
I.II.III

Men dance with mad men
as the drinking continues unabated
The Devil feels useless
because the revelers have no need for Baphomet

The mistress is found,
the wife befriends, bends and licks -
She can taste her husband
in the burgundy parlor

The women in full blush -
A nude painting of Huldra smiles
from above the fireplace;
her loins burn the doings of the burgundy parlor

Outside the nymphs wash in the brook,
preparing for the ephemeral celebration -
the wailing woman
who drowned her children in the river
dries her tears,
lays her burden down;
she removes her dirty white dress
with a laughter that gurgles from her throat
As the nymphs wash her body
the wailing woman lifts her arms to the heavens,
forgiveness,
no more sorrow,
no more regret,
The women join hands in laughter,
skipping playfully to the celebration

Now the men are gone...

Fear of Woman
the old woman dismisses her reservations
She retrieves the violin from behind two lovers
in the burgundy parlor
She plays the 24th caprice
as the nymphs give her wine through a straw

All women are exquisite, talented
pieces of music,
sexual acts,
Nothing flaccid about the performance
So much vigor coupled -
the tightness of the violin strings,
the enormity of the cello,
third handedness of the viola
& the tinkly ivory of the milky piano keys

The food begins to dwindle,
Huldra performs her miracles –
bread, olive oil, fruit & more wine
Lust turns the pale wine burgundy
The women don't mind,
partners are changed again;
the waltz continues;
more wine imbibed –
the coming of spring dreaded

Now Hera arrives,
blood on her hands,
blood on her chin,
blood dripping down her neck –
She removes her laurel wreath,
opens large brown eyes and smiles gently –
Father Zeus is now a eunuch
Here's a glass of wine Hera
Huldra descends from above

The two goddesses walk hand in hand to the river
They remove their vestments –
The blood is washed away,
They slowly make Love,
And the spring...
the spring...
it never comes......

Lay Your Hands

Elizabeth lost her family. Visitations with her three daughters were supervised. She moved in to her ailing father's garage. Empty bottles strewn, the mattress smelled of piss. General Relief kept her in cheap whiskey.

In the mirror – emaciated frame, sunken face, dirty blonde hair, dull green eyes. A bottle of stolen Old Crow, three long drinks and the desire to be taken, to be ripped apart in waves of want, in the dirge of despair. Elizabeth walked to Echo Park Lake – at least she wasn't living in a tent by the water. Another drink of the Crow; the nausea of her thoughts. Below an Evergreen Tree, right hand reached for a rusty box cutter from her Rising Sun Bomber Jacket. Death to the Crow! A larger than usual drink – Her left palm turned towards the grey in the dull firmament.

"Your last chance…. I can't fuckin' take it!"

The murmur of the 101 stopped. The birds warbled as if the break of day. A little Mexican girl with the contrast of olive skin and white flowery dress materialized. She silently offered Elizabeth a smile and white Lily. The flower retrieved, box cutter fell from her hand. Elizabeth wept; asked forgiveness – *"Que la paz esté contigo."* The little girl laid hands on the kneeling, whimpering woman. A chorus of unseen spirits whispered prayers in Gaelic – *Lorica.* Together – little girl and diseased woman walked home.

The night brought convulsions, secretions, bloody stool, bloody screams – the dogs snorted, howled from sex with the neighbor's sow. The bed moved, the windows opened and shut, demons pounded on the exterior walls, the large crack across the ceiling began to drip – Elizabeth scratched at the walls violently until her fingertips lost their nails and became counterfoils of encrusted blood.

"I am no more… I am no one!"

The morning star rose. Water, coffee, cherries, nicotinic acid left beside Elizabeth's bed. Her bloodied hand reached for water, bit the cherries, licked the pits – niacin with coffee. A new vibration – Elizabeth stripped, ran outside, arms extended – the summer heavens boiled with rain! Elizabeth inundated herself, dancing in full circles, laughing in violence – the current of the heavens set her aflame!

The days continued to arrive. In the mirror – the sultry vigor of curves, a stare ready to be returned, ready to accept invitations. The world became green. The sow next door gave birth to strange looking pigdogs with curly tails, brownish noses and long pink ears. One evening Migly, the runt pigdog of the litter, got attacked by a hawk with black talons. Cut, bleeding – Migly's intestines steamed on the ground – Elizabeth rushed over, closed her eyes, laid hands on Migly's twitching, gushing little pigdog body; Migly's tongue began to vibrate. Elizabeth opened her eyes to find a completely healed pigdoggy licking her flower painted toes.

Elizabeth struggled with the healed Migly. What manifested the heat emanating from her hands? Perhaps all in the imagination?

Elizabeth searched for wounded animals. On a small bridge on Glendale Blvd., a dirty little white dog with a burned eye wagged his tail. The filthy little dog trembled as it looked for scraps among the boulevard waste. Elizabeth approached, closed her eyes, laid hands, healed the dog – both eyes bright and hopeful!

Elizabeth walked to the shopping center to procure cases of water; she laid hands on the bottles then rolled the shopping cart to Echo Park Lake where she cured addicts. When all were gone, Elizabeth dropped to her knees and gave thanks; the little Mexican girl in the white dress smiled from behind a dying palm.

The profligate addicts of Los Angeles came to Echo Park Lake. Elizabeth restored their spirits; healed the trauma and pain. Contortion and yelling, screaming and out of place laughter suffused the park. Once out of their cocoon, people smiled, played games and embraced. They said their goodbyes and returned from whence they came, to reestablish their lives with the imperfect people that encompass their family.

Abattoir of addiction – succulent morsels of abuse, the penury of people's pain now a wealth of wisdom – Elizabeth felt strong, satisfied and proud. She began to accept courtship from the materially wealthy. Soon, Elizabeth owned a two story Victorian on Carroll Avenue; she brought Migly home and built him a three foot tall Cedar wood dog house replete with canisters of different pig delicacies. Although the supervised visitations had been softened, her daughters had yet to come over.

Evenings spent regaling; the nights began in elegance, ended in Dionysian debauchery. Migly sopped the often spilled drinks. The pigdog was a charming, sexy drunk to some of the more adventurous women. He paraded in a black bowtie tonguing the few words he learned in English from the party guests.

Elizabeth met James at one of those gatherings. James preferred wines of springtime and eternal promises – charcuterie at Portuguese Bend Palos Verdes. Silk scars tied to the bed, unsafe words, hips became pieces of pounded meat, the hunger of lust, angry pleasured faces, a bruising, sticky concurrent climax. American Spirits for Elizabeth, Paso Robles Reds for James.

Elizabeth's daughters refused to visit; they preferred public places. Dissatisfaction, boredom. The half pig, wealth, healing powers and orgasms became metronomic. Something lacked. Even the earned respect and reliability both needed to fuck off! Elizabeth walked into the kitchen and opened one of James' wine bottles. What excitement returned!

"Here's to a miserable two years without you baby!"

After the third bottle, Migly walked in with his curly tail and cute little bowtie. Somehow a knife drawer opened beside Elizabeth. As Migly was hunched over drinking from his water bowl, Elizabeth grabbed his long pink ears and slit his stomach open! Migly's pigdog eyes cried blood. His left hind leg kicked for a bit while his intestines steamed.

Elizabeth opened a fourth bottle and lit a cigar. She walked to the small bridge on Glendale Blvd. The little white dog with the bright eyes approached her. She bent down and licked his snout. In a sudden rage, Elizabeth grabbed the wagging tail and burned his eye with the palpitating cigar! The little dog ran furiously, falling off the bridge onto the traffic below.

Cigar in the right, Wine in the left, Elizabeth laughed all the way to Echo Lake Park. She sat under the Evergreen tree to continue the celebration. At the far edge of the lake, the little Mexican girl whimpered. A shadow, nine feet tall, began walking slowly around the rim of the lake. The water agitated, resembled ocean waves. The little girl ran in horror. The cloaked figure walked towards Elizabeth. Three feet away, but she couldn't see his face – only the glowing red of his eyes. An offering – the shadow figure extended a wet, rusty box cutter and a bottle of WhistlePig.

Venice

The house quiet – the usual noises absent. The footsteps echoed. I stepped on a toy that will soon be donated or thrown away. The grass tall; the dog kept alive by the generous neighbors. I contemplated an exit with no energy to execute. Many messages received yet no visits. Only my elderly mother knocked at the door.

Always happy to see mother yet I never expressed it to her. Instead, I'd point out her shortcomings. Stoically, she'd listen to my complaints – asking forgiveness for her faults. She'd quietly weep then ask what I wanted to eat. The silent washing of the dishes and clothing. The swept floors unnoticeably cheered me. In her departure, the sign of the cross – a quiet benediction. She left and the drinking escalated.

I couldn't sleep on the bed. The couch by the window became my only refuge. I'd open the windows and curtains to stare at the infinity above – the first noble stirrings in my heart; philosophical treatises on the nature of existence. "Trust the Universe" seemed to be the overarching theme.

The evening knock at the door – the papers formally served. Mind twisted, heart clenched, a tall glass to make it through. To whom do I run? I wanted to leave. What entity would like to hear me scream? No exertion – only the soundless subjugation of the spirit. I can't embrace the delivered Bibles. The distant prayers aren't working. I walked outside in the hope of seeing anyone.

Two older ladies with funny hats grinned at me – I nodded back with blurry eyes from my porch.

Another cold drink – the only warmth left. Something awful kept traveling inside. How do I release this parasite? Forever present even in the joyful times. Perhaps I'll drown it. Three more drinks and at least it slowed. The temptation to stab it out – if only it would remain still. Suddenly, I felt like walking.

Gray hope in my perambulation. At least I wasn't angry with happy people. I encountered an older lady wearing a shawl and rosary beads. We both smiled gently. The Slum by the Sea greeted me. The touch of evil gone. Neptune washed ashore Doors and an Addicted woman named Jane; great gifts from the Southern California Ocean gods. The purple charm almost gone – too expensive in Venice. The corporate Freakshow rearing, walking hairy ass first to the bank.

The ocean whispered its motivation, its openness to comfort. I extended my arms against the wind and moon – heart beating at three-four with the deafening waves. Ocean Witch walked on water without wavering. Her purple robe dry. She embraced me as I knelt before the moon. A few kisses atop my shaking, crying head; chest heaving against her purple robe with the inlaid golden stars of majesty.

The morning sun in the east. The parasite awoke, swimming through the pain in my hungover head. What to do next? Another bottle but just enough to calm the circumstances.

The realization that I became bored – I asked and it was given. Beautiful woman – charming, fit, intelligent, witty – it didn't matter, she became familiar. I looked elsewhere and even the deception lost its savor. Eventually, the crumble. The mask came off. The air to my face nauseating; the parasite swirled around the left temple of my face.

I'm not sure I'd want her back – six months. Should I try again? The sudden urge to become healthy, happy….convivial. I switched to wine because Mediterranean cuisine keeps you vigorous. Large servings of salad, fresh fruit and fish. Every evening a long walk after dinner. I began with a half a bottle of wine, three quarters – a full bottle consumed by five. I had a drink in the morning along with black coffee and toast. I consumed vitamins at the urging of my mother. It's not the alcohol that kills you but the nutrition deficiency. I smirked with tolerance because I've hidden a half bottle of whiskey in the garage behind the pictures of my daughters.

I think I want her back? I had an early dinner, only one bottle of wine and plenty of fresh water; crushed garlic and vitamin C for stamina. I started to walk by the salt water. Bewitched, a young woman with a triangular tattoo on her wrist smiled at me. Her blue-grey eyes contrasted with olive skin. The fragrance of roses, lavender and strawberries encircled her dimpled cheeks and light brown hair. Although a few feet away, she looked distant. I had no choice but to follow her into the store with the eyes and triangles. Her long purple dress caressed my wooden spirit. She looked over her shoulder and smiled again – more lavender and strawberries.

I'm surrounded by books, rocks, herbs, statues, eastern quotes – western guilt. Here, Christ is not King but senator. The blue-grey eyes with olive skin sat at a peculiar table; she shuffled large cards with pictures. She doesn't gesture, doesn't ask me to sit. I'm attracted to a small statue of a woman on her knees kissing a butterfly. I made my way to the table. She looked up to show her dimples as I sat.

"Cut the cards wherever you want."

Baphomet stared – his right hand raised in allegiance, hairy crotch, eyes on his knees, Roman numeral fifteen, inverted star – woman and man horned in bondage.

"What does that mean?"

"Let me finish and I'll explain everything."

The cards rested on the wooden table. Blue-grey eyes looked at the formation then closed her eyes and whispered. I waited patiently for the verdict. She rose from the table, locked the doors, drew the curtains and retrieved three red candles. She lit the fire on the three wicks with a wave of her right hand. The flames flickered like writhing tongues whenever I heard hissing. The back room called, beckoned.

"You need to unleash the Shadow, the hidden side of your psyche. I can sense your fear. Your reluctance is causing addiction, attachment, pain. Let it go. How can I help?"

"Grab two masks from the wall then let me enter your back room."

She grabbed two Venetian Carnival Masks from the wall; the Jesters Blue and Gold, Red and Gold. We entered the low lit room – closed the door behind. Three lamps in triangular formation against the north wall. My hands on her hips, she braced against the east. I slowly lifted her purple lace dress, began at her ankles, caressed her thighs – the tips of my fingers barely touched skin. I pulled her toward me at the bend. I continued to gently trace, carefully avoiding the building silk between her legs; I teased the outer edges. Her hips began to respond, a slow tremor, underwear torn off, she gasped for air – strawberries, roses, lavender in the room – the butterfly screamed.

"Did you feel the Ocean inside of me? I'm the daughter of the Ocean."

"I met your mother yesterday. She was very kind to me."

"My mother has great compassion for men in pain."

"Nothing seems to satisfy me. What if I want to die?

"You are dying. I felt death in your release. I saw Death over your shoulder laughing at how seriously you take life. What is hurting you so much?"

"My wife left and I don't know what to do. The uncertainty....."

"It hurts that your wife left?"

"Yeah"

"Then let it hurt!"

Then let it hurt! Those words penetrated. Blue-grey eyes and I embraced before I left. The Boardwalk void of pedestrians. I called to my Ocean Mother for guidance into the wine colored water. Her shadowed outline as she walked away from the gibbous moon and onto the sand. I hide myself underneath her silky purple robe. She is stern, stoic, strong! A caressing of my longer, unkempt hair. The redness of her compassionate heart against the black and gold of her garb.

Awake! The next morning to the coffee and wine. I felt the parasite begin to calm. The succubus on my bed, beckoning, writhing, still asking to be touched. I've started skipping breakfast. I spent half the day in headaches the other half tending to nosebleeds. I find out my wife is dating another man. The parasite grew and moved more prominently and deliberately; it is no longer satisfied with wine. I procured a single-malted Scotch whiskey. The parasite finally gave me rest.

Many mornings bleeding and numb. The parasite stronger, more agile. It now travelled up my neck, swimming in the blood around my face. I could feel the parasite when I pressed against my cheek. I was waiting for the parasite to travel to my thigh or some other place where I could cut it out with a knife. Many hours I sat drinking, watching the parasite's movements, waiting with a knife in my hand for the perfect opportunity.

The parasite settled in my throat. It remained in the left side of my throat for days. I was worried it was laying eggs. I bought a large bottle of whiskey then drank half of it in less than five minutes. Before the flood of alcohol dampened the electricity in my brain, I took a knife and cut the parasite from my neck. I bled profusely yet managed to stop the bleeding by wrapping my neck in an old shirt. The pink, veiny, bleeding parasite squealed, flopped on the floor. I poured vodka into a fish bowl then placed the squealing, bleeding parasite into it. It swam in the vodka; the parasite calmed and so did I.

The parasite grew to four inches into a half leech, miniature pig that squealed whenever its cloven hooves attached to the rim of the fish bowl. It seemed perfectly content swimming in vodka and consuming its own feces. I watched it swim for hours envying the energy of the pig-leech. I couldn't lift my arms from the sofa. The rattling in my chest began. I knew what was happening and accepted my fate.

Suddenly, the pig-leech started squealing uncontrollably. Flutters of purple butterflies entered the window. The scent of lavender, strawberries and roses permeated the decaying stench of the room. The fish bowl caught fire. The pig-leech, thrashing and screeching in its fiery bowl, began to bleed green. Blue-grey eyes extracted the pig-leech from its bowl and stomped it with her bare left foot. I sat motionless, feeble – unable to react. From the bedroom Baphomet stared – his right hand raised in allegiance, hairy crotch, eyes on his knees, Roman numeral fifteen, inverted star – woman and man horned in bondage.

Ocean Witch entered my home. She smiled long at the chaos, stepping over the dead pig-leech, then entered the bedroom were Baphomet waited. The bedroom door shut. Blue-grey eyes began to clean my home. I heard chanting, laughter and joy emanating from the kitchen. Baphomet exited the bedroom then slowly walked out the front door. Ocean Witch and Blue-grey eyes carried me to the bath. They washed me using lavender soap. Once done, they carried me to the bedroom where clean white sheets and open windows waited for me. I breathe deep and stretch my tired, emaciated body. Blue-grey eyes entered with strawberries, chamomile tea and a smile. After a few minutes, I too began to smile. After feeding me, Blue-grey eyes undressed.

"What happened to your mother? Is she still out there?"

"Mother left a little while ago."

"I wanted to thank her."

"I can thank her for you. What about your mother? Did you ever thank her?"

Blue-grey eyes and I talked through the night while listening to the roaring ocean. Naked and vulnerable, we returned to the laughter of childhood. In the morning, she kissed me on the cheek then departed.

I looked at the calendar realizing I was served six months ago. The old feelings began to come back. An hour later, I heard a knock on the door. Mother entered and gave me a quiet, Catholic benediction.

"Mom, I want to say…."

"There's no need son."

I fell to my knees. Mother embraced me. I am loud – I screamed, wailed, grunted, and cried until I settled into a soft, calm mood. Mother brought me a pillow and warm blanket. I slept the gentlest sleep. In the wee hours I heard three beautiful women in the kitchen sharing and laughing. I opened my eyes and they raised their wine glasses to me…

"Go back to sleep."

Father

For a brief moment there was hope. The neighbors conspired and bought us a small turkey; father had been gone for three days. Mother, sister and I walked to the local supermarket to purchase a humble amount of rice and beans to go along with our turkey. Our walk was sprinkled with laughter as we talked of pleasantries, good memories. On the way home, I carried the rice and beans and mother the *Coca-Cola*. Even though we were very hungry, we'd become accustomed to ignoring the pangs. When the hunger became unbearable, we drank sugar water and that usually stopped the salty tears. Tonight we break bread as a family.

Today was a new beginning! I secretly wished, though would never confess, that father never return. As I walked, I kicked pebbles and smiled reservedly at the promise of a peaceful and abundant Thanksgiving. Sister reached for my hand and we both began to skip together, swaying the bag of beans and rice to and fro. Mother laughed, watching from behind, taking extra care as we crossed the street. I always enjoyed walking with mother and sister. The difficulties of life were minimized on those long walks.

As we approached home, we immediately knew something was wrong. The front door hung, almost parallel to the ground, sustained only by the lower hinge. The dogs barked and howled at the clatter coming from inside the house. As we entered, my father sat on the kitchen floor, clutching two bottles of empty wine. My mother frantically ran to open the refrigerator.

"Are you looking for your fuckin' turkey?" asked father loudly with mocking concern. "Here you go!"

He flung one of the empty wine bottles, shattering it against the wall near mother's head. Mother fell to her knees crying, understanding what father had done to the turkey. Sister and I embraced mother and cried too; I wanted to destroy him.

"That's right you bitch, I traded the turkey. Happy Thanksgiving! Next time you treat me with disrespect, remember there are consequences! I'm the father! I'm the fuckin' husband! I'm in charge! Not you! Not any woman! Understand?"

Father then stood, bearing down on us as we huddled on the floor whimpering. As he walked out, he took one more kick at the front door, completely unhinging it from the frame. As father walked toward the gate, a very large pig attacked him. I ran to help defend father; the pig obeyed when I asked it to leave. Father didn't say thank you. He just eyeballed me with drunken contempt before leaving.

Mother received the call two Thursdays later as sister and I did homework. Father was hit by a bus as he stepped off the curb. Mother asked the neighbor lady for a ride to White Memorial Hospital. Although our last encounter with father was scary and violent, I prayed for his injuries to be superficial. When we arrived at the hospital, the neighbor lady took sister and I into a waiting room as mother inquired about father's condition. Almost an hour passed without mother coming back to report on father's state. The neighbor lady told us with a wagging finger to remain seated while she found mother. A few moments later, the neighbor lady came back and gestured to come with her. We obliged and knew something was wrong by the way she held us close as we walked toward our crying mother at the end of the hall. Nobody had to tell me – father had died.

There was no funeral for father. I didn't get a chance to say goodbye to his lifeless body. There was no reconciliation, no peace, no spiritual awakening that finally set father sober. I'd been left with unanswered questions for the rest of my years. I prayed for the impossible opportunity to have a candid conversation with father. The pain palpitated, masked into a clenching, unforgiving anger.

As the years passed, my sister Sandra moved away to live with relatives in Grady, California. Although I too was invited, I refused to leave Los Angeles. I had very little money and knew Grady would provide stability – but I didn't want "stability" – I wanted Los Angeles. My mother had been placed in an asylum somewhere in Norwalk because she insisted my father still came to visit her. I'd remind her that father had passed.

"No! Your father came yesterday. I don't want you to get angry but he slapped me across the face… not too hard though. He knew not to hit me with a closed fist. I begged him not to leave. I swore I wouldn't call the police but he still left."

"Mom, the fucker's gone!"

"Don't speak about your father that way! Show some respect. I know he's gone but he'll be back."

"No mom, fucker's gone for good. Dead! D-E-A-D! Dead!"

I really enjoyed putting the words "fucker's gone" together. I liked the fact that it made my mother sob. I hated her for tolerating him for so many years. Even dead, she's still putting up with his bullshit. My father never demonstrated any desire to quit drinking. He never apologized or tried to make amends. Why is my mother still hurting over this complete and utter jackass? She claims to hear and see him in the hallway. In her warped illusions, he is sober and speaks of responsibility, forgiveness and family. I'm more inclined to believe that father appears as a ghost rather than the assertion that he talks of responsibility. When alive and drunk, my father talked grandiose business plans with great fervor and even greater gesticulations. I'd sit at his feet enthralled with his ideas, completely convinced wealth was inevitable. The truth is my father never had any money. He had no desire to put any business plan into action. My father was so irresponsible with money that he was even afraid to open bills. My mother managed the money; she was the one who had the courage to open the bills and deal with them.

We sold the house to pay for mother's stay at the asylum. The house was bequeathed to father after the passing of Grandfather Lecubarri. My grandfather fled the Basque countryside during the Spanish Civil War. Most refugees went to other parts of Europe and Latin America but grandfather insisted on Los Angeles. We settled in Boyle Heights.

Before selling the home, I tried cleaning it but to no avail. I hate to confess it but it was just too painful. The strange thing is the good memories filled me with the most sorrow. Our family came to an end so abruptly. Had they been real? Father, Mother and sister where gone. I was left alone to tend to the last responsibility pertaining to our immediate family. I missed the three of them. Yes! I missed father too. I stared at the bent trash can father warped with a swift, generous right kick. I walked from the kitchen to the bathroom and reminisced, with painful nostalgia, at the times mother gave sister and I warm baths. One time, when father wasn't too inebriated, he played Glenn Miller on the record player. The music sounded so good that I started dancing! Father clapped along loudly, laughing, enjoying while mother smiled big in the kitchen. Sister ran in from her room and joined in with some funky steps of her own. Soon, all four of us were dancing in the silliest of ways.

I put my fist through one of the shoddy windows in the living room. Although the blood dripped profusely down my fingers, I simply didn't care. I took my left fist and punched out another window. As I stared at my bloody hands, I realized the anger had only wounded the sorrow. The ugliness lumped heavy in my chest. I tried to cry but the tears evaded me.

I awoke with a massive headache and dried blood on my arms. I dreamt that all four of us went on a tranquil autumn walk around the neighborhood. My spirit was betraying me. Why would I dream such fantasies? The sorrow was still there, accentuated by the pain in my arms and the dreams in my head. I lay still while reality flooded back into my mind and heart. When I turned left towards the kitchen, I thought I saw father leaning against the door smiling at me mischievously. Instead of getting angrier, I simply smiled back at the vanishing image. Perhaps mother wasn't crazy after all.

I fled the home never to return again. My buddy Fenix helped me hire a Realtor to take care of the sale of the house and the subsequent transfer of money to the asylum. I drove mother to the asylum with only the clothes on her back. I tried, in vain, to explain to her the reality of her situation. Mother was more interested in the turning color of the leaves on the trees. The asylum looked peaceful with its manicured green grass, abundance of neatly trimmed trees and old Grecian benches. I envied mother. As we pulled up to half moon driveway in front of the hospital, two beautiful, kind nurses helped mother out of the car. I stepped out but remained close to the vehicle. As they started escorting her into the hospital lobby, mother turned around and waved goodbye behind the tall glass doors. I waved back with my bloody right hand and smiled graciously even though my heart was blackening. I parked the car and decided to take a walk around the grounds of the asylum. Going on walks always seemed to calm me. I sat for a moment on one of the benches hoping for some type of release. It never came.

I drove back to Boyle Heights. My friend Fenix asked me to come over after I'd dropped mother off. Fenix offered to come with me to the asylum but I refused his kindness. Instead, I asked to borrow his car. As always, Fenix welcomed me with a calm, stoic, friendly demeanor.

"Everything good with your mom?" asked Fenix as I handed him the keys.

"Yeah. The place looked cool. Lots of trees. Nice grass and flowers."

"Sounds good. You ok?"

"I'm good."

"You want to take a drive? I kinda want to get out of here."

"Yeah. Let's bounce."

That was the extent of our conversation pertaining to my mother's placement in an asylum. I wanted to talk about it, confide in Fenix the horror I felt inside, but nineteen year old young men from Boyle Heights don't "confide." We drove down Mott Street, past Roosevelt High School, and eventually took a right on Brooklyn Ave. Without Fenix indicating it, I knew we were headed to Evergreen cemetery. We entered the gates slowly, turning right and parking underneath a large, shady tree. I enjoyed wandering through the old graves with their statues and symbols. Evergreen cemetery boasted the internment of prominent families; rumors of ghostly apparitions accentuated by the strangeness of the last names encircling the grounds. Once fatigued, Fenix and I settled into his vehicle underneath the shady tree.

"What happened to your hands?" asked Fenix.

"Got pissed. Punched out the windows."

"Don't you think you should probably wash them? They could get infected. They have a restroom right by the entrance."

"Fuck it. I'll wash them later."

"Cool."

Fenix reached behind my seat and opened a small cooler. He never needed a bottle opener. Fenix was a genius in many ways especially the opening of beer bottles. He popped a beer with the metal part of his seatbelt then took a long, gurgling drink that emptied half the bottle.

"That first drink is always the best," sighed Fenix. "You sure you don't want one?"

For two years I'd been saying "no." I'd sit there smoking cigarettes while Fenix drank. When he got too buzzed, I'd drive us back. Watching my father get drunk and beat the psychic and physical shit out of our family made it easy to say "no" to drinking alcohol. Fenix never pressured me. He offered because he was polite and always shared. Fenix was never a mean or violent drunk like father; he became more sociable. I began to wonder if my perception of alcohol was skewed.

"Fuck it. I'll have a beer!"

Fenix reached for the cooler and popped another beer – this time with his lighter. I grabbed the beer with my clotted, bloody hand. It felt cold against the injury. I took a drink – didn't like it very much. Fuck the first drink! This stuff tastes like shit! Fenix noticed my scowl and began to laugh.

"You don't like it or what?" asked Fenix with one eye closed and half a grin.

"Yeah, love this shit! Can't you tell? How the fuck do you drink this shit?"

Fenix didn't respond verbally. He smiled at me and lifted his eyebrows. He was on his third beer and obviously beginning to feel the effects. I took courage and chugged the rest of the beer. Fenix nodded his subtle approval. I felt uneasy at first but then let out a long belch that woke the maintenance worker resting against the neo-gothic chapel. My face started to feel warm. The pain in my hands and heart subsided almost imperceptibly. I asked Fenix for another beer. Again, he nodded in approval. This bottle he opened with a ring he wore on his right hand.

"Enjoy this one. No need to rush," suggested Fenix.

I took his advice and drank this beer in three rather than two drinks. Upon finishing the second, the first fully caught up with me. It was my first time drinking alcohol. I started to feel a sense of calm. My family problems drifted into the periphery. I stared and marveled at my hand and the fact that my brain controlled it. I kept clenching and unclenching my right fist – fully fascinated with the human body. I wished father had a tombstone. Sometimes I'd cry on it and sometimes I'd piss on it. Speaking of piss, I had to take one. I walked behind the chapel, enjoying the cool breeze on my warm face. When I returned, a third beer was waiting for me in the cup holder. I made quick work of it.

"You wanna go get some more or you're good?" asked Fenix.

"I'm down."

We returned ten minutes later with a small bottle of vodka. Again, we wandered the cemetery grounds on foot, bottle in hand. Drinking at a cemetery is much smarter than drinking at a park or any other public place. People are in mourning, they're expected to drink. No one ever asks questions. If they do, simply point to a grave. You mourn, deal with death. People know better than to question the cultural habits of grievers. Lamentation and woe are as Universal as alcohol and cigarettes. Take my advice – drink at cemeteries.

Alcohol turned my nightmare into a type of beautiful, sonorous requiem; the world painted blue instead of red. The graves reminded me of the utter foolishness of life. I drank the last fourth of the vodka and soon all became nothing. I rested with the dead – supped with annihilation. I awoke to the moaning of a woman adjacent the neo-gothic chapel. I searched for Fenix but didn't find him. His car was still parked in the same location. I recognized the unease I felt as thirst. How can that be? I stumbled to the water hose and drank. My body regained strength after I watered it. As I looked closely at the car, I realized Fenix was sleeping in the driver's seat. I staggered to the Chevy and passed out in the back seat.

The next morning, we drove out of the land of the dead. I thought of father. I'm convinced father thought life pointless, meaningless. Why else would he forsake us? Alcohol saved my life that day. I wasn't hopeful but I was alive and found a way to deal with pain. What type of life could I expect? I'm convinced some people just aren't meant to lead sane lives.

Fenix's parents, in their infinite mercy, offered to let me live in their garage. I'd have access to an illegally built restroom attached to the outside of their home. I regret not expressing more gratitude towards Fenix's parents. I certainly felt thankful; I just had difficulty communicating it.

Boyle Heights – Victorian homes, dog shit and trash in the parkways, brain and tripe tacos in red and green sauce, soulful Mexican families, loud mufflers, cars driving too fast down residential streets, murals of the Virgin Mary on liquor store walls to prevent graffiti. Most neighborhoods in America are interchangeable; Boyle Heights – inimitable biography.

Fenix's parents gave me a mattress, lamp, small table and wooden, dilapidated chair. To ease the loneliness – I drank, smoked and read. The Benjamin Franklin Library was only a few blocks away. I travelled the fucking world with only a library card. I couldn't understand why some people didn't enjoy reading. I remember teachers begging morons at Roosevelt to read. Somehow I knew the ignorance of these idiots was willful, deliberate. I stopped going to class and started reading at Evergreen Park. At the park, nobody told me what to read. I didn't have to write some formulaic five paragraph essay upon completion of a book. There was no grading, no morons being forced to read – just me and the author. Writing an essay on Socratic Dialogues would've fucked up the entire experience. Fuck "comparing and contrasting"! I'd have grown to loathe Plato if I had to explain, in a five paragraph essay, why Euthyphro felt compelled to prosecute his own father.

When Fenix came home from work, we either went out to drink or stayed in and drank. Fenix also read voraciously. The irony regarding our love of language is that we spoke in muddled, dispassionate fragments. We were thrifty, concise with words. We'd drink and lift weights on Fenix's rusty, spider ridden bench. My hands still hurt from breaking the windows but I didn't care. Lifting weights, like alcohol, helped me forget. Although I didn't express it, I don't know how I would've survived without the kindness of Fenix and his parents.

I continued to bench press while smoking a cigarette. I could tell Fenix had something on his mind. Whenever he wanted to talk about something, he'd nod to himself. I had the suspicion he rehearsed not only the words but the gestures. Fenix was meticulous in his communication. He never spoke unless he actually had something to say.

"My parents think you should get a job. They're happy to have you here but they think you should work," uttered Fenix.

"You know anyone hiring?"

"At the restaurant. I'll ask Fernando. I think they need a dishwasher."

I nodded in agreement.

That settled it. It made sense to me. I should be contributing too. I'd gotten so self-involved with my own problems that I failed to consider the needs of Fenix's family. Besides, it'd be nice to have some cash in my pocket.

Saturday evening came. I showered and got dressed. Although I shampooed my long hair, it was still a tangled mess. I never brushed my hair. As long as it didn't stink, I was good. I wore a white Led Zeppelin Swan Song shirt and black Levis. I didn't like wearing all black. It was too predictable. I also didn't wear any bracelets or nose rings or any of that other shit. I kept it simple. Some people just try too hard.

While waiting for it to get dark, I started reading the introduction to the Meditations of Marcus Aurelius. The librarian at Benjamin Franklin recommended the book. She thought I'd be attracted to Stoicism – she was right. By the time Fenix knocked on the door, I'd finished the introduction to the book and three beers. I was ready. Fenix smelled ready too. If I had three beers, he must've had five.

We went to a backyard gig in City Terrace and that's where I met her. Madeline – beautiful, smart, funny – down for anything! We talked books and music; we shared beer and cigarettes. I started working at the restaurant with Fenix and managed to save up and buy a 66 Chevelle. Madeline hated Santa Monica Beach so we'd drive to Venice. She'd pack a picnic – beers, sandwiches and books. Madeline never wanted to plan anything. She relinquished control to the untamed Universe and to my surprise things always worked out! We met many cool, humble people. We'd experience the most interesting, stirring things.

One summer morning, I received a call from Madeline telling me she wanted to go to Venice beach that night. I told Madeline I'd pick her up after work at 9 p.m. She instructed me to pick her up after 1 a.m. Fenix overheard the conversation and smiled.

"I'm happy for you bro. Madeline seems cool."

"She is. Hey man, just wanted to say thanks for helping me out."

"No worries. Hey, ask Madeline if she has any friends."

"I will."

"Beer?"

"Why would you ask something stupid like that? Hell yeah!"

Fenix and I had many beers and showed up to work buzzed. Don't need to be sober to wash dishes. I began to wonder why Madeline wanted to meet so late. She never failed to keep me interested – never allowed the mystery to be satisfied.

I finished work, drove home, lifted weights, ate pastrami, showered, two beers, read Alan Watts, got dressed then drove to pick up Madeline. She lived in an old Victorian in El Sereno. Madeline walked out of her house holding a large leather box painted with red symbols. I got off to help her carry it but she adamantly refused – wouldn't let me touch it.

"So what's in the box Maddy?"

"You'll see!"

Maddy's mischievous grin.

"I'll see? Let me see now, just a little peek. C'mon, what's in the box?"

"A message."

"A message? From who?"

"Stop! Just wait until we get there."

We arrived at Venice Beach a little past 2 a.m. Although it looked heavy, Madeline wouldn't let me help her with the box. We found a secluded spot away from the Boardwalk. I began to feel uneasy – admittedly scared and angry. Madeline noticed; she knew me well. She asked me to leave for a short walk while she set up. Madeline also suggested I don't drink until after we are done. I paced the Boardwalk unexplainably anxious. I began to get angry at the box. I wanted to kick the box, throw it in the ocean! Fuck, I wish I had a beer to calm down. I heard Madeline's voice call to me.

Madeline's arms outstretched towards the moon. She stood in the center of a candled circled. In front of her, behind the southernmost candle – a book on the sand. Madeline asked me to enter the circle. I felt fear, sorrow and anger. I couldn't move. I just watched and listened to Madeline recite words. When the candles flickered, I began to see the outline of figures just outside the circle.

"Someone wants to speak to you. It took me a while to figure out who it was. He kept showing up. I know how you feel about him so I was reluctant. I hope you don't get angry with me baby. He just wants to speak with you."

"Who is it Maddy? I don't see anyone."

"Look to your right."

That's when I saw him. I could only see the top portion of his face but it was undeniably him. In a low, crestfallen voice I heard:

"Son, I'm sorry."

I fell to my knees and began to weep. I could feel his hand on top of my head. All the ugliness inside began to disperse, carried away by the tumultuous wind of the Pacific. I heard him cry:

"Son, I'm sorry."

I looked up to see him one last time. Father looked at peace. The candles extinguished. Madeline got on her knees, embraced me and cried with me into the twilight.

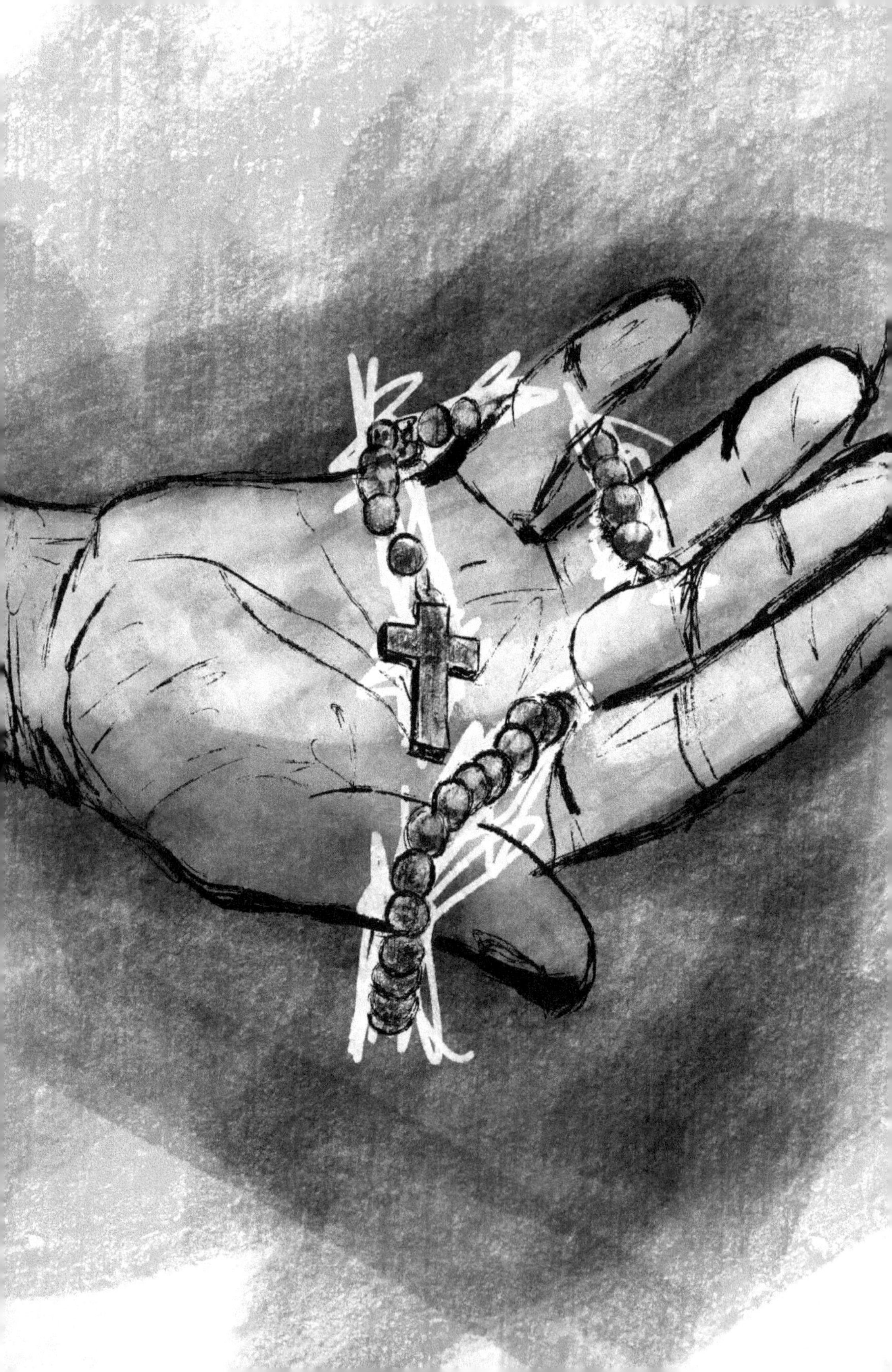

The Bridge

I've made my prayers, conducted the sacrifice – elements bring forth the promise. The unseen vortex in cascades of red watercourse. Three cuts on my left palm stopped amidst the bloody, flaming candle. A lambent shadow assumes its own will. The window erupts with intent and fury! It is released......it is done!

"Oh great Master, I thank thee!" *extinguish......*

The anticipation kept me awake in flowery darkness. I manage a couple of hours dream sleep. Resplendent, on a bed of Madonna lilies, she waits for me –fragrant floret coupled with the fire in between. Heaven in her eyes, Hell everywhere else.

The morning ritual – the conclusion of musk. I exit my dorm; at the edge of the classroom, in the periphery – Beauty walks in late. She is the answer – the beginning and end. Wait! Did she just turn to look at me? Is it starting to work? A deep breath to calm the punctuations of my heart!;?

A celebration beneath the purple rain at the sculpture garden. Again, they are filming something. I raise my vodka tinctured glass in veneration to the Wrathful Deities. A seven foot, muscular, bronze woman stares at me – arms at her hips. Here comes the deeper warmth of the Russian water. A wayward statue enunciates her arrival. She penetrates my third eye with her stare. From conviction to fear, her gaze flutters when she looks behind me.

Blurry blonde brunette figures and their eternal giggles. Young women learning to stimulate the top of their triangle in long strokes and circular motion. The energy wavering, building – faster, more pressure –the flood of good feelings and the honest, unnecessary shame. Fuck, I wish I had a little more to drink!

"Here you go?"

"Who are you? How'd you know I wanted more? Did I speak out loud?"

"No, but I knew. Drink up!"

"Thank you Sir. What do I owe?"

"You paid this morning. Let me know if you need anything else."

He walked away slowly, tipping his hat to a tittering strawberry blonde. The bottle already open:

За любовь*!*

Fade to Black

Where am I? My pants are wet! I crawl from under a bench to the hose for a drink of water. It's already dark. Shit! I missed two classes. I wonder if she noticed. I'm sure she noticed! There's a little left in the bottle. Enough fumes to get me to the dorm. I take the last drink and drench myself. Better to be soaked from head to toe.

The next morning a slight headache and renewed sense of purpose – long shower, meticulous teeth cleaning, fresh clothing, parted hair, exit. The drumming of my heart in a steady two-four time of anticipation and desire. I entered the classroom to find she is no longer in control of her gaze; she turns over her right shoulder to unequivocally look at me. I feel an ache, nostalgia, coursing blood surging in adolescent places. The doubt and anxiety rise – the insecurity – a virus strain resistant to contracts with Old Scratch.

Here she comes –

"You think you can help me with something?"

I nod yes.

"It's the strangest thing. You sure?"

Another nod.

"Can you rub my shoulders while I write my paper this evening?"

Third silent nod.

"Meet me in front of Powell at 6?"

"Ok," the first word that dared.

I skipped two classes and spent the rest of the day preparing. Ten minutes before 6, I began my walk to Powell. Again, she is early. We find Seclusion waiting for us at an eastern corner. She opens her book bag and lays out her materials across the table.

"Get behind me and don't stop until I tell you," she whispers over her shoulder.

I stand behind, move her long ginger hair aside, and begin – softly, slowly at first.

She turns to look at me, "Can you do it a little harder?"

I try but the cuts on my palm begin to hurt. I use my elbows and right hand; her soft moans begin.

"Right there! Keep circular pressure on that spot!"

This ethereal beauty drops her pen, closes her eyes and continues low, whispered moans. The taste of blood, the dissolving feeling in the legs, the urge to destroy in order to create. Possession – materially, spiritually – soundless violence in our veins!

"Use both hands."

"I can't use both. My left hand hurts. See."

"Which one of those cuts am I?"

"The purple one."

"Let's go to your dorm and take care of that center wound."

A short walk to the dormitory – we go inside. On the bed, Beauty gently pressures my left hand. The cuts begin to bleed. She stares – I want to run! More bloodletting, she crushes my hand and starts to tickle the center cut with the tip of her tongue. My body weakens, my breathing labors – Beauty continues flicking vigorously until I collapse. On the floor, she removes my clothing. I try to fight so she ties my limbs to the furniture. Her eyes two slits of vertical red; she lifts her skirt and mounts. I'm afraid to reach peak for fear of disintegration. I've no choice. Faster, harder – the hurt then sudden release – I'm flying low above rising flames – return to Earth. She cleans me with a wet towel, unties me, smiles from above. Beauty reaches into her book bag and hands me a bottle of Beluga Gold Vodka.

За женщин*!*

Fade to Black

I awake a little past 3am; the smell of lilies pervasive. Beauty gone but a thin, well-dressed gentleman on the edge of my bed. I still felt the effects – surprised to be alive.

"Who are you?

No answer. He lights a cigarette in the darkness and I see his face for a second – it doesn't look right. I must be hallucinating. He takes a long drag and I think I hear a snort.

"Sir, please tell me who you are?"

"We met yesterday by the two candles."

"I only had one candle."

"I had a second one lit on the other side."

"What other side?"

"You summoned me. You bled on the flame of the candle facing west. I've given you what you want. I'm here to collect."

Another drag of the cigarette.

"That wasn't what I wanted."

"No? You wanted the woman, you got the woman."

"I wanted her to be my girlfriend – to go hand in hand to the Village Theater, Musso and Frank, the Lost Sunken City in San Pedro."

He chuckled and snorted – looked at my drained, bloody hand. Another cigarette lit, another glance at his face. I know what he is now.

"Are you a child lost in the fiction of Hollywood?"

"I feel sick! Look, my hands are trembling. Can I have another bottle?"

"I'll give you another bottle if you bite off my snout." Chortle.

He leaned into the flame of his lighter.

"Shall I kneel so you can reach my face?"

He took off his *saturno – cappello romano* – slowly. Kneeling next to me, he tends close. A compulsion, craving in my canines! The breath smells sulfuric and sweet. My head lifts violently and at once I have his snout clenched in blood and pig fat. His child-like laughter at my vehemence. My teeth cut and I spit blood and snout across the room. He sits back on the bed and lights another cigarette – smoke swirls from the gaping hole in the middle of his face.

"Very impressive – did it taste like bacon? Ha ha! Here's your Stolichnaya."

I drink to wash the taste of salt and snout in my mouth.

"Can you let me out of the deal? I'm sorry I invoked you."

"You didn't invoke me – you released me. You lowered the dam and now you want the water to return? Didn't you enjoy her? I was watching. She was incredible! Not that it matters now but she was into you long before I showed up. You just didn't have the courage to approach. Drink up!"

"Why didn't you tell me she was into me already?"

"It doesn't work that way. I eliminated the risk for you and now I'm here to collect. Finish the bottle. I have more."

За встречу*!*

Fade to Black

The morning trickled in from the side window. My strength was beginning to return. I keep thinking of the rope in my closet. Still some vodka left and another bottle on the stow. No sign of a snout. The room in a breeze, in a cold that eddies around the exposure of my skin. My left hand begins to bleed. I open the drawer looking for cloth and find a rosary. *Now and at the hour… save us from the fires of hell!*

I begin to weep. Tears, blood dripping ceaselessly. *Poor banished child of Eve.* What have I done? Who can help? I call my friend Ismael. He asks me to drive to his home in Pasadena this evening. Through the day on my knees with no response. Nightfall arrives and I leap onto my Chieftain Classic Indian motorcy-cle. I get off the 134 and start racing down Colorado Blvd. I see strange lights from underneath this ostentatious, ancient bridge. I stop to look closer. I hear voices murmuring "join us." I can't decide. The antique lamps watch and grow brighter. Two large pigs appear – snorting, growling, they run at me from either side of the bridge.

Fade to White

Non Serviam

Wendy was aroused in the early morning hours by strange warmth emanating from her lower body. Her breathing became heavy, punctuated with little moans. Wendy attempted to reach down and investigate but a force suddenly pinned her arms back. The moaning grew louder, her muscles began to spasm, the harder she fought, the greater the waves of desire – climbing, climbing, complete – release……slow descent!

What was that? The doctors surmised benign sleep paralysis. What about the presence? What about the scratches on her back? Wendy's fiancé abandoned her once he saw the marks. Wendy declared a moratorium on relationships. She attended to the sacrament of confession next Saturday evening.

"In the name of the Father, and of the Son, and of the Holy Spirit. May God, who has enlightened every heart, help you to know your sins and trust in His mercy."

"Amen. It has been two months since my last confession."

"Please tell me your sins."

"Father, I am losing faith in the church. My mother recently died and with it my belief in God. I have difficulty forgiving those that have harmed me. I feel anger in my heart and I wish ill upon people. I don't understand these feelings. Therapy hasn't helped. I just feel something awful inside of me."

"Is there anything else? I'm sensing there is more."

"That's it. There is nothing more."

"You say you're losing your faith yet here you are confessing. There is a part of you that still believes in the Mercy and Love of our Savior otherwise you wouldn't be here. I'm sorry for the loss of your mother. She was a good woman – came to Mass every morning at 7. Give yourself time. It's natural to question one's beliefs especially when a loved one passes. Anything else on your mind?"

"I'm kind of embarrassed to talk about it."

"The trust and sanctity of the confessional is absolute. God already knows the trouble you carry in your heart."

"Then if He already knows why confess it?"

"You don't have to. It just helps to unburden the spirit to verbalize the worry and suffering you feel. I can also help provide guidance."

Wendy paused. She began to tear up. The priest was patient.

"Father, like I said, I feel embarrassed, ashamed even but I have to tell someone. Before mother died I began dabbling in the occult. It all started innocently. I read the Book of Thomas. I know the text is considered apocryphal but the words fascinated me. That led me to The Sophia of Jesus Christ. From there it spiraled and descended to places that I…… I don't know how to put it in words…… injured my spirit? Something felt wrong, something definitely felt off but I couldn't stop! Some unseen force kept pushing and prodding me towards these texts and other things."

"What other things?"

"Casting spells, incantations, even ……sacrifices."

Wendy began to weep openly. The priest gave her time. After she calmed, Wendy continued.

"We sacrificed pigs in the mountains of Pasadena near Strawberry Peak. We then used the blood to conjure certain spirits. The last time I participated, I refused to kill a small pig. The animal just looked at me with such large, beautiful, painful eyes Father. I just couldn't do it! Everyone became upset. They threatened me with possession because I had broken the circle. No one outside our covenant knew what we did in secret. My fiancé didn't suspect. These rituals occurred during weeknights when he was at work."

"Do you still participate in these rituals?"

"Not anymore but there are certain spirits, powers, ramifications that still linger."

"There is no greater power than the blood of Christ. In your struggles always remember that."

"I will Father."

"Our society denies the existence of evil. It lays flat the reality of the spirit entrusted to each and every one of us. Your spirit felt an admonition when you participated in these rituals. You hurt innocent animals and lied to the man you love."

"I'm scared Father. They know things about me."

"Can you elaborate?"

"I have a healthy sex drive. I was very participatory in the rituals involving sex. I enjoy being dominated, pinned down. Sorry Father, I don't want to share too much considering your vow of celibacy."

"It's quite alright. You may proceed."

"Are you sure Father? I don't want to make you uncomfortable?"

"There is nothing you can tell me that I haven't already heard. Please proceed."

"I love being dominated. My therapist says it stems from my sexual assault in college. I was forcefully raped by a classmate in my dorm and as a result, I had the most powerful orgasm. I felt ashamed because I had an orgasm during my assault. I didn't want to orgasm. My body betrayed me. I certainly didn't want to be raped. Now, I don't enjoy regular sex and I can't seem to reach climax unless there is an element of coercion, of being forced and conquered. I've had trouble sharing that secret desire with my partners but I shared it with the covenant."

"Rape leaves terrible trauma and injury. It wasn't your fault. How your body reacted also wasn't your fault. You're still processing a horrible event coupled with the death of your mother – you've been through too much. It is only natural that you seek answers and question your beliefs. Your heavenly Father understands and forgives if you are heartily sorry for all your sins?"

"I am."

"Ok. Through the ministry of the Church may God give you pardon and peace, and I absolve you from your sins in the name of the Father, and of the Son, and of the Holy Spirit."

"Amen."

Wendy came home to her evening solitude. She went for a run, practiced yoga, read her novel, ate her salad, then sat in a warm, candlelit bath. Her condominium by the La Brea Tar Pits was minimally furnished, clean, impeccable. She moved in after graduating USC four years ago. Wendy loved the condominium except for the writing she discovered in the master bedroom closet.

"This is where it all went wrong"

Wendy quickly painted over the writing but, no matter how much she painted, the words would reappear. Sometimes, swarms of large flies would infiltrate and sit perched on the closet hangers. The more Wendy tried to kill the flies, the more they would multiply. Wendy called an exterminator; he found no entryway or logical reason for a periodic fly infestation.

One Sunday morning, as Wendy was showering, she heard heavy footsteps in the hallway. All doors were locked and the alarm was still activated. Wendy frantically rinsed the soap from her hair, turned off the water, then listened carefully; three more footsteps outside the bathroom door and a low growl. Slowly she opened the door and a horde of black, thick cemetery flies invaded! Wendy ran to her front door setting off the alarm. Her neighbor Tom came out of his condo and found Wendy naked, dripping wet. Tom covered Wendy with his jacket. They inspected Wendy's dwelling and found nothing out of the ordinary; no flies, no strange footsteps.

Wendy dressed while Tom waited. Later, they attended Mass, visited LACMA then had a long late lunch. Wendy searched her mind for other things to do before finally deciding it was time to go home. At the pharmacy Tom bought a bottle of Grey Goose and red solo cups. Wendy drank – hoping courage would arrive before she got home.

Tom was gone – Wendy alone. All the lights turned on except for the malfunctioning Christmas lights across the banister. They flickered whenever Wendy walked by. She reached the connecting outlet at the bottom on her knees in an attempt to reset. The Christmas lights burned so brightly after reconnection that some shattered. Wendy felt two hands grab her hips from behind; her legs weakened – again, she felt the warmth in her lower torso. Her hair grabbed violently, subjugated, dress and underwear torn. Those waves of heat began again. Wendy felt a ghostly hand reach around. This became the catalyst, the beginning of the powerful release; the spasms of an unconnected body moved in force of pleasure – in possession of pain.

Her body betrayed her again. Wendy sat pinching the bruises on her right thigh. Deep, unsubstantiated laughter coming from the bedroom. She knocked on the wall connected to Tom's condominium. He arrived and sat on the floor with Wendy as she explained what happened. He suggested visiting a hospital – concerned more for her mental health – but Wendy insisted they go to the Cathedral Chapel of St. Vibiana on La Brea. She took an empty water bottle.

When they returned Wendy and Tom sprinkled the condo with holy water. Tom's degree in biochemistry made him a believer of facts and proof – repeatable, quantifiable phenomenon. Wendy opened the closet in the master bedroom and the sulfuric smell emanated became punitive. Tom searched for the origin of the odor to no avail. The water bottle was suddenly ejected from Wendy's hand; Tom's biochemical brain confused, picked up the bottle of holy water to examine – a slow, low growl – the bottle forcefully thrown from his hands!

Whispering…"Do you believe me now Tom? I don't know what the hell is going on!"

"There has to be an explanation."

"Let's go for a little walk – calm down. I could use another drink. Liquor store?"

"Yeah!"

Wendy and Tom returned with beer and a small bottle of tequila. They sat on the floor of Tom's condo drinking, talking about what to do next. Tom grew braver with each drink and smile from Wendy.

"I say we just go confront it! A bully needs to be confronted. It'll back down once it sees our resolve."

"I have a Ouija board. There was some writing on the closet wall when I moved in. I can't get rid of it no matter how much I paint. I've been curious. Can we ask it some questions? Maybe if we understand what it wants, we can better persuade it to go away. What do you think Tom?"

"However you want to do it, let's just go do it!"

Tom and Wendy each took a large shot of tequila before returning to the infested condo. The Ouija board is retrieved from under the bed. Candles are lit – the Ouija board rests on top the bed – ready to be played. Two fingers each on the planchette and the slow circles around the board begin.

"Who are you? What do you want?" asks Wendy.

No response, no movement.

"You keep touching me; forcing me… what do you want?"

No response, no movement.

"Tom you ask it some questions."

"Why'd you throw the bottle from my hands? I'm still not sure you exist. Give me proof! Are you scared of being confronted? Are you a coward?"

Tom suddenly felt a powerful, painful burning on his back. Wendy took him to the restroom to inspect. Tom had three long, thick scratch marks across his back. Tom didn't want to leave the restroom with the bright lights. Somehow, Wendy's tilted head, exposed neck filled him with courage. They sat on the bed and continued their interrogation of this hostile defendant.

"It must be easy to attack when you know I can't defend myself. What do you want?" asked Tom.

The planchette begins to move. It spells out: GO AWAY.

"I'm not going anywhere until you stop attacking Wendy. What are you?"

GO AWAY

One of the candles turns off. Wendy gets up to light but it won't stay lit.

TURN ON

"I tried to turn it on. Can you stop touching me? Can you stop pinning me down?"

TURN ON

"Do you know why there was writing inside the closet? Did you witness what happened here?"

EVIL ONLY EVIL

Wendy suddenly fell on the bed and started to laugh uncontrollably. The crucifix on the anterior wall fell. In the candle-light, Tom sees only the white of Wendy's eyes. He purposefully blinks three times – translucent cloaked figures surrounded the bed.

In a sweet voice, "Can somebody pin me down?"

The candle that refused to be lit now dances in flame. The cloaked pig faces turned to look at Tom. In the closet the grunts of pig crashed against the door. Low moans and a certain writhing on the bed. Tom is forced into the closet with the biting, devouring pig. A knife appears at Wendy's side. Cloaked figures remained patient. Wendy arises – she bloodied the knife with Tom and Pig. Wendy tears her clothes with the bloody knife. The cloaked pigs take turns in her pleasure.

EVIL ONLY EVIL

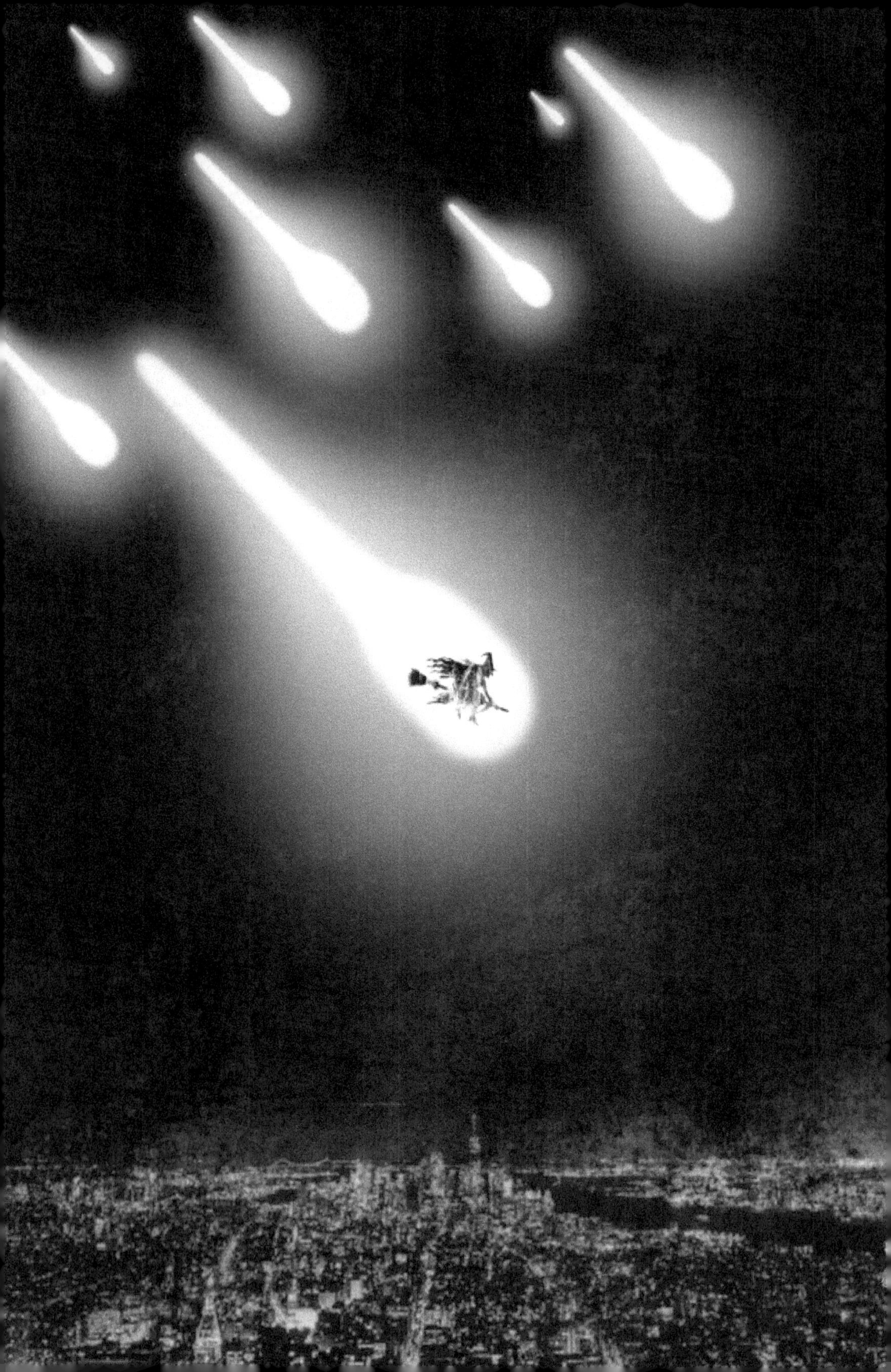

The Witches of God

A walk through a dark wood
New Moon
Light still radiating
It follows me – no!
It comes from me – emanating, pulsating
From deep inside

I see the entrance to a cave
Covered in moss and dangling vines
Inside four women wait for me
I embrace each and give thanks
-gratitude-
they simply nod-
no words, no sound

I continue to walk inside the cave
Another opening inside, more narrow, darker even
Yet I continue to illuminate the darkness
The next room is full of people
They are all me…
From girl to hermitess
I greet my adolescent self
Still irreverent, still curious and angry
The old woman picks up the crying child
She waves me off with a smile –

I continue into an even smaller, narrower opening
There a green light glows –
matching the light from my chest
I enter – I AM no longer
I'm part of the green energy
It pulsates, hums, gives life, gives warmth

A concentration of energy
I'm jettisoned through a tunnel
Into the Starry Night Sky
I explode....
Ready to become again....

To the cave the women enter; foreign rants and foreign chants to the conformist community. You think God your religion? Circling eternal, the cauldron has no starting point. So the women choose a place and begin again. The soul unburdened at the four corners of Corral Canyon.

"Let's take off our masks and pretend that we have true faces to hide," gleefully exclaims Xiola.

"Take my mask – I've grown tired of my face," says Dolores.

"Truth is the ice water of the holy," asserts Amy.

"Then lies are like a warm bath of evil?" asks Grace.

The ceremony is fire – reminiscent of Jesus' descent; souls being set free. The traditions of Gehenna… Courir de Mardi Gras. The Defenders of nature –unmasked nudity, sweating thighs and breasts. Hope resurrected, grave clothes removed – "Rise" the women chant "Rise" – a great Phoenix from the cauldron – burning fire wings, smoke encircling all strict divisions of the city. *God* speaks to the current generation. The relics in boxes they call churches drip blood. No more pleasantries, no more logic, no more forced laughter. The skirt is lifted. The woman that beats the human heart lifts her unctuous shroud.

"I baptize Los Angeles in Fire & Whiskey,'

The recent corpse of Peter at the corner of the cave is brought to orgasm by the tightness of Dolores; silky, slithery, sex on the Sabbath. To the spirits:

"Oh figures of yesteryear and tomorrow, release us from all that is sorrow. Exultation and dance we give, that all who have died soon will live!"

The four women howl, scream, dance… a horrible wail that scares the patriarchal Satan. Dolores scrapes her bloody fingernails on the floor, Xiola beats her head against the wall, Amy scratches her thighs vigorously until they bleed, Grace bites at her bottom lip until it drips with saltiness. Exhausted, they hold each other – weep, mourn, become one with loss and sorrow. Pain is release, Pain is life.

The heart no longer beats to the rhythm of trauma. Hope has entered the ceremony with her warmth and purple ascendancy. The conundrum of fear and faith acting in unison. The work may now commence. May God have mercy on his city full of "Angels".

Flying through the city – the four forms of power diverge to conduct their duty. Xiola descends on the arrogance of men – pins them down, back and forth, harder and harder – they beg, "Please stop!" – enclosed in a sarcophagus of sin, treachery and pride. In orgasm, spirit is ripped from body. Dolores takes these laden, pewter souls and flies them back to the Sacred Cave. There Asmodeo waits; his bifurcated tongue extends to swallow. Amy carries the rigid corpses to the westernmost hilltop of Griffith Park. White fire from Grace's palms sets aflame the cadavers; immediate and complete incineration. Thirteen men consumed…

Back to the cave to further pleasure Asmodeo. Three erect penises, Amy and Grace on knees, Dolores on groin and Xiola being brought to with bifurcated play. All five orgasm at the tethering of 3:33 AM, summoning the great protecting Spirit of the city. A great immigrant Hog on hind legs dances in Fives around the cave. The Witches of God kneel; the cauldron seethes, fire from the eyes and snout, Asmodeo growls in ghastly delight, drinking the warm Whiskey of the Crows.

"Hail, Hail to the Holy Hell. Arise my dead sisters. The beast gives permission; no more acts of contrition. Come now and reveal, the spirit humanity tried to steal – with his dogmas and order, we expel the religious hoarder!"

Great hog starts to moan. The thirteen spirits of the deceased men are regurgitated by Asmodeo. Hog speaking frenzied tongues. Scanning languages until he settles on the West Germanic: The Great Hog of Los Angeles speaks:

"You must kneel and lick my four daughters. If you bring them to, I will release you."

The thirteen men's tongues thrashed. Seven jettisoned through a tunnel into the starry night. The green energy revolves around the fantasy of good and evil. At the top rim of the triangular, darker eternity, they witness the forgiveness of Satan.

Fire! The four daughters reach climax, Four Fireballs spinning ad infinitum. At the break of sound they exit, spiraling fire onto the central coast of California – into the vineyards with the labored allegiance to Mary. The sleeping workers watch the flames in the distance. Stripped, the four women celebrate the new wine. Always a circle, aflame the night sky adores through its luminous full moon. Energy, a trapped winemaker rewarded lasciviously for his generosity to Dionysus. A large crate of burled wood, fresh grapes turning to inebriation a city that is loved by the strangers, the home of the unwelcome. All abodes and surrounding boundaries receive the gift of Dionysus. All are compelled to drink by dark matter. The city of Angels rises in debauchery and joy. None are harmed because the heart is opened fundamentally. The rule of Gold truly applied to the rejected ambers of the evil flames. Women aflight, uncaring but not cruel – Father now forgives and loves. Unconditional is his surrender to the warmth of the family. Now, night slowly leaves into the rising redness of Helios– remnants of bliss, ashes of beauty!

These nights, the Witches of God rejoice. To the masks, the habits and veils they return. Tonight is the ceremony of the red vestments – the Feast of the Martyrs – to the Monastery of the Angels the four masked women return and Asmodeo and the Great Hog drink Whiskey to the West......

twas ever thus.....

The Landlord of Downtown Los Angeles

Father left when I was six, mother died soon thereafter. The next few years are a distortion. I recall pain, but not sadness – shame but not regret. At fourteen I entered Roosevelt High School. I never attended class but lost myself in the cannon of books readily available at the school and surrounding libraries. The history of mankind plagued with a circle of suffering, spinning, taking turns on unsuspecting populations; perspective, I counted myself fortunate. I decided to continue.

I attempted to make friends but had no interest in sports or anything outside of books. Solitary, I wanted companionship but on my terms. The blades of the outcasts lost their sharpness. I ambled the streets of Downtown Los Angeles, trying to circumvent the bums, trash and smell of piss. It became a game – trying to find a decent crack to read my books peacefully.

"Sir, can you spare some change? I haven't eaten in three days!"

I'd look up from my book and simply stare until they left. I tried being polite but it kept them begging longer. My rhythm lost, sometimes I couldn't continue so I'd look for another place to read. The nicer areas in Downtown like Bunker Hill or the Financial District never welcomed me. I wasn't dressed offensively nor was I dirty yet they always asked me to leave. I couldn't read at home in my trailer because my Uncle was on disability and always drank excessively and played loud, loathsome music. I was relegated to the shittier parts of Downtown Los Angeles with the bums, trash and smell of piss!

Vista Hermosa Park is where a bum with a grey beard actually threw piss on me! What disturbed most was the destruction of *The Book of Lies*. Instead of ending his life, I sat there seething, simmering, sulking. He walked away unscathed. My hands juddered with rage yet failed to enact rightful, holy revenge! I still think of him and remember his features very distinctly!

I met my first companion Jack outside the Central Library. He was interested in the book I was carrying. A shared bond – kindred – solidified, strengthened straightaway.

"Where do you find quiet Jack?"

"At home."

"Must be nice."

"You want to come over? There's plenty of space and Landlord is a good friend."

It was formerly a four story orphanage. I moved in after a couple of weeks. The place afforded stillness and spent it lavishly. Silence here was sacred and practical. The location served as some type of headquarters. The Christian garb and iconography confused me; it seemed upside down, irreverent, yet perfect to the atmosphere. Jack became my roommate. He watched the blank walls for hours mumbling equations, oftentimes laughing.

His garble was foreign; words with phlegm. Maddening mixed with amusement.

I removed Christ from his nail on the anterior wall. He refused to speak. What waves of remorse before this instrument of death – still no flutter in the heart? I envied the expression of sorrow and pain. At least he felt. What archetype follows? Will we be hanging images of a man in an electric chair in two thousand years?

At night, I'd walk the long, darkened hallways. Devoid of light, I used my other senses. No shoes for fear of noise. My hands caressed the concrete walls descending the passing of each doorway. The Sisters prayed rituals in their ancient language. The lost children wept quietly. Envy crept. What sweet release. I wanted to go.

At the end, my instincts sought the west. A candle in a stray room. A barely perceptible man in a brim hat motioned. I ignored his request to enter the candlelight every time. I'd no desire to follow instructions – I'd no curiosity for the contents of the room. Every night he beckoned. His face I never saw. He gesticulated again towards the room. What tenacity and persuasion of shadow creatures.

The women began to whisper as I walked back. In the assembly of voices, I recognized my mother. The creeping was slow and deliberate. I ignored the manifestations. They reached for me knowing I couldn't be touched. I opened the door to my room leisurely. There was Jack staring at the wall at three in the morning. I burned a candle – ran my fingers over the flame. He laughed at the dancing shadows. Christ wore the same upside down expression.

"Jack, who's that man at the end of the hall?"

"That's Landlord. He wants to meet you."

"I guess I should thank him for letting me stay."

The next evening I accepted Landlord's offer to enter his candlelit room. He lit two more candles then we sat and talked. His face was kind, almost gentle looking. He poured cask whiskey into two small, iridescent glasses.

"We always drink in moderation young man. Is that understood?"

"Yes… understood (slight nod). Thank you for letting me stay. I enjoy the quiet very much."

"You're an avid reader. We're all readers here in our sanctuary. We challenge ideas, traditions, compliance, preconceived notions. Words give power so long as you read the correct books."

"And what are the correct books Sir?"

"The ones that warp the illusion of a structured society. They're the ones that contain the Truth."

"Where do I find those books?"

"You're already reading them. You naturally gravitate to those books because you're one of us. You are home my son."

The Landlord smiled and my face contorted into a half grin.

"Sir, is there anything I can do to repay you for your generosity?"

"Contribute and participate in the group's activities."

"I will."

The fourth floor housed the rituals and oral traditions; it had no windows and was entirely soundproof. Jack invited me to join the ceremony held at seven o'clock each night except Sundays. Hitherto, I politely declined but was now ready to accept. Thursday evening, I waited at the staircase that ascended to the fourth floor. A beautiful olive-skinned woman with penetrating eyes stood beside me.

"I'm not sure what happens in there or what I'm supposed to do."

"It's your first time?"

"Yes. I met Landlord recently and he graciously asked me to participate in the group's activities."

"Well I'm glad you're here."

"What is your role up there?"

"I'll give you a hint – I'm menstruating."

"I don't know what that means."

"You don't know what menstruating is?"

"I know what menstruating is I just don't know how it pertains to what happens up there."

"I guess you'll see."

The ceremony lasted one hour. I now understood the role of menstrual blood in the ritual. The Landlord gave me an undertaking, instruction to solidify my initiation. Jack and Christopher were assigned to help carry out the order given by Landlord.

We exited the building near midnight. The three of us walked the outer edges of skid row. We waited patiently for the correct person. Christopher smoked nonchalantly in the dimly lit, trash filled, piss smelling alley. An alignment, a Jungian synchronicity. The perfect person was approaching. I recognized his features clearly.

"Can you guys spare some change? Hey can I bum a cigarette?"

"Give him a cigarette yeah? I want him to have one."

Christopher looked at me strangely.

"Here."

"Can I have one for later too?"

"There is no later."

"What? Hey wait.. don't I know you from somewheres?

"You do. Vista Hermosa Park."

I grabbed him by the beard; Jack taped his mouth. Christopher his hands. Down on his knees. Two fists from above; blood dripped down his eyes and nose.

"Hold him Jack. I have to wash the blood from his face. Piss is sterile right?"

Now someone else smelled *my* piss! Old grey beard here even tasted it! I unsheathed Landlord's blade – two in the hamstrings, three in the calves. We left him whimpering, hogtied.

A return to our sanctuary. I hand Landlord the bloody blade; he reacted with barely a smile.

"Get some sleep gentlemen. I will see you tonight at the ceremony."

A gentle, deep, long sleep. I awoke in the late morning to find Jack mumbling at the wall. Special clothing had been laid out for me by Bianca – the princess of the sacraments – vestments, long and purple. My day spent meditating, reading, fasting. The hour to prepare arrived. Bianca silently walked me down the corridor to a bath prepared with Rosemary leaves and Grape Hyacinth. By candlelight, she undressed and joined. Climbing, climbing, climbing Climax – completion – she collected what she needed for the ceremony.

Willing participants –adults outside the common, illusory boundaries. Hail to the prophets! Even Landlord kneeled before the Lord of the Angels. Arms and wings outstretched! The mixture of white and red in the ceremonial cup. Women danced in red glory, ardor, energy, nudity, ravishment – Dionysian cavorting, pig heads no longer snorting, Landlord levitated six feet above altar and decreed:

"Roam the city of Angels and bring her converts to me.

"Here it begins……

"Here it will end……"

Penultimate

A certain call, an incantation, a mocking retreat
– frantically searching for peace
The eye of God stares as it takes its final gasp
Apotheosis, cynosure – all wealth, prestige and pleasure –

I don't think I can continue

The raw, bloodiness of my fear do the demons feast
Berashith – I am the Universe ready to regenerate this
disgusting world
Study the Sacred Sigil
A few things to do before the final exit

Of course there is confusion
You thought this world easy?
There is no New Age
Only fecund buried thought fruiting under new gods

I am open to all!

Forget the fetid limits of the soon forgotten church
The service sends a Babylonian Whore
Depravity, Depravity – the abominations are center stage
The trumpets will soon be sounding

May you decipher the hidden meanings and
find your way home
The words are coming alive;
crying as bloodied babies fresh from the womb

Los Angeles is the holy Jerusalem; Jerusalem is the unholy
Los Angeles

The Doctrine of Last Things

What forms have we manifested? Under what auspice? The lost days continued to come. I reviled the ancient church with its circumstance. Outside the gates – blackened – the wings fluttered and flew to the steeple covering the same full moon that watched Jesus in the Garden of Gethsemane. The pigs swam back to the land; Legion once again possessed. My hands weakened as the blood began to drip from inner palm and wrist. I envied the truly insane. Why do these women follow me?

To the beach of St. Peter. The tide pools low. The women beat their bloodied heads against the rocks. The pigs begin to feast. A symphonic growling, harmonized, accented by the dropping of the heavy waves. The fire angels of the city circle the scene. From above, they are merely spectators – audience members. Now the fornication. Evolved pigs in cloaks descend the hill, masquerading as men, find stumps and pieces of the leftover women to fuck. The ocean rises. The ceremony is complete. The water baptizes the scene back to purity – no elements, no trace – only the recollection in mind and spirit.

A pig mask washes ashore. The mirror can't stand my face. Let's pretend I'm somebody else. Racing – my mind, please slow down! Perhaps I missed some of the details. There were pigs and a host of other things? Blood drips into the Pacific. The sun is cut, wounded, festering from what it can see in the ocean.

"My Lord with what audacity I raise my prayers to You. My heart is full of sin and my mouth just spoke evil. My soul is infected and my faith dwindles. In shame I raise my arms. Forgive me. I have fallen. I humble myself before thee."

A cloaked chimera approaches; from under the robe a bottle of Old Crow. Sweet relief at last my Lord! Thank you for the answer to these images. The normal hell returns. Pedestrians, parking meters, bickering couples, angry motorists – people on their way to work. I alone am triumphant; in the moment …..I AM; in the moment I drink. How must they envy me!

The call I received stillborn. The waves inside unendurable. Oblivion, please oblivion! I kick the pebbles on the street. "Maria what can I do?"

"Whatever happens we'll figure it out together as a family."

My child with the blackened eyes. Only a few breaths. I carry him to the ocean for St. Peter's blessing. Release, to be resurrected. My child floats towards Terminal Island. The sun flashes like an old Hollywood camera.

Oh sweet nightfall! No stars, new moon, the City of Angels a blackened grid. ….

The great California earthquake – locusts, the sixth angel, the number of the beast! Here comes the pale horse descending from the sky! The women drunk on blood, the men on lust! The prayers for immediate death! The beast is captured and flung horns first into the Pacific. Now the murdered children, eyes completely black, walk out of the womb of the water. The crucifixes in their hands sharpened, held upside down. Another great earthquake – the ocean moans and howls, writhes in white virginal pain; more blood at the shore. The water recedes further than the human eye.

The children begin the slaughter. Organized, meticulous, stoic – the cleansing of the earth in blood! The gift of life in its circle continues. The Lake of Fire cut open with crucifixes in Downtown. All are thrown including you and I. He has given up his image. The fire angels of God lift Satan to his earthly throne. The Kingdom of heaven is removed from man's heart. As in the beginning, the great formless void, the darkness, the face of the deep… and the SPIRIT OF GOD no longer hovered over the face of the waters.